NEUROPOLITIQUE

NEUROPOLITIQUE

Timothy Leary

with
Robert Anton Wilson
and
George A. Koopman

NEW FALCON PRESS • 1991 • SCOTTSDALE

International Standard Book Number: 1-56184-012-2
Library of Congress Card Catalog Number: 88-81431

First Falcon Edition 1988
Second Printing 1991

NEW FALCON PUBLICATIONS
7025 E. 1st Ave. Suite 5
Scottsdale, Arizona 85251 U.S.A.
(602) 246-3546

"I've written a book . . . containing all of my work of the last six years. I believe I've solved all our problems, finally. This may sound arrogant but I can't help believing it. I finished the book . . . and two months after was made prisoner. I wish I could copy it out for you; but it's pretty long and I would have no safe way of sending it to you . . . I will publish it as soon as I get home.

Ludwig Wittgenstein to Bertrand Russell
from prison, March 1919

The Tactics of Evolution are:

Space Migration
Intelligence Increase
Life Extension

The Goal of Evolution is:

Fusion
(at higher levels of intensity
acceleration
aesthetic complexity)

Neuropolitique

This book is dedicated to:

Bob Dylan
voice of his time

and

William Gibson
voice of his time

Table of Contents

Table of Contents

Table of Contents

Table of Contents

Introduction

The first version of *Neuropolitics* was written during the years 1973-76. At that time I was held prisoner by the Nixon regime. Several of the early chapters were composed during periods of solitary confinement.

I must confess that at this time I was alienated, a bit daft and given to occasional fits of irritation. So color the first version of this book indigo—as in jail-house blues.

Rationally and basically I was content, even proud to be an ideological prisoner. I understood how the game of Major-League Professional Philosophy is played. I knew that throughout history those who invented concepts and new paradigms too effectively and too publically tended to be waved to the penalty box. The folks who control the prison keys invariably dislike dissenters, conceptual innovators, libertarians, reality agitators.

Free thinkers, especially the charismatic, become extremely unpopular, not just with the Ruling Party, but with that majority of the population who do not think for themselves and are irritated when confronted by jazzy new ideas.

As many of our philosophers have learned, lengthy prison time does give one a different perspective on politics. A certain cynicism develops. You realize that you are either "in the system" or you're an outlaw. One realizes that (except for small Scandinavian-type nations) every law & order bureaucracy operates the same way. Soviet admirals think exactly like our naval officers. German narcs are programmed to think like our DEA agents. Having been arrested in four continents I can testify that cops and jailers are pretty much the same all over the world. They have the power and they use as much as they can get away with. American jailers are not allowed to be as brutal as those in some other countries, except in small town jails in Mississippi . . . or far-away places like Mai Lai. Prisoners tend to be the same the world round. Their real "crime" is that, for one reason or another, they lacked the power or intelligence or money to keep them out of jail.

Lawyers and civil service workers also tend to be the same around the globe. Like many convicts I became peeved at all lawyers, both for the prosecution and the defense. They all profit from the crime-punishment industry. Often the attorneys for the poor defendants make much more than prosecutors. The term "criminal lawyer" is too often a tautology.

My hero, at this time, was a grumpy Russian philosopher named Alexandre Solzenitsyn. I read and reread his books about the "Gulag Archipeligo," the Soviet system for silencing dissenters and compared them with what I was observing around me.

Solzenitsyn wrote:

Introduction

"Only those can understand us
Who ate from the same bowl with us."
Or, as Waylon Jennings sang it, "We received our education in the prisons of the nation, me and Sol."

It was Solzenitsyn who made the reckless claim that one writer telling the truth can bring down a regime. And he made it happen! His writings were so powerful that he was finally released from the prison that is the USSR and hustled off to Switzerland. The world media instantly surrounded his house in Zurich. Do you remember those scenes when he came out and shook his fist at the TV cameras? How strange that he should be unfriendly to the western press which had elevated him to heroic stature. I sympathized. He probably felt the way I did when I wrote the first section of this book. A bit embarrassed at being used as an unwilling cog in such a primitive, simplistic sin-crime-punishment-media machine. I'm sure Giordano Bruno felt the same sense of indignity when the Inquisition popped him into the micro-wave oven.

But all that's in the past. Now, March 1988, I have cheerfully eliminated the sections of this book which expressed, often unfairly, my incoherent annoyance at lawyers and media stars, supposedly in the friendly camp, who had not "eaten from the same bowl with us."

I hope those at whom I railed from jail will understand. I particularly regret my whining complaints about Bob Dylan. He stands as the single most powerful, eloquent voice of his generation. I have dedicated this version of *Neuropolitics* to him and made him the hero of my first novel, *What Does WoMan Want?* (Falcon Press, 1988).

This said, I can add, in all candor, that there were some excellent concepts and moving passages in the first prison version. Way back there, before Jobs and Wozniak had made the computer a personal mind-appliance I was groping to describe the cybernetic world that is now being described and realized by William Gibson and Ted Nelson and Jaron Lanier and Eric Gullichsen and the other cyberpunks.

And the proposals which George Koopman and I made for financing and constructing space colonies have become a hands-on reality here in 1988. Koopman's American Rocket Company is launching its first space "jeep" in the summer of 1988.

So, to use the baseball metaphor, my performance in writing this book had some solid hits and many misses.

I no longer feel embarrassed about the enormous number of boring or stupid or nutty concepts I launched in the 38 years I have been performing philosophy.

Introduction

Here's why.

Performing philosophers in the Information Age are like baseball players. The best homerun hitters also strike-out most.

The more innings you pitch the more wild pitches and walks.

In the feudal and industrial ages the production of new paradigms was a different business. Back then philosophers marketed one or a few original concepts in a lifetime and defended them against attack from rival theorists. Success was determined by academic approval and bureaucratic acceptability.

In the Cybernetic Age the professional assignment of a performing philosopher is to produce new paradigms which will inspire and encourage others to think for themselves. Today philosophers do not give people food for thought. They teach people how to think, how to conceive themselves. Philosophy becomes do-it-yourself linguistics. How many neo-logisms and thought-hybrids have you conceived this month?

Over 38 seasons I have written thirty books and hundreds of essays/interviews. A paper-trail littered with thousands of new ideas.

I have confused many people, myself included, because I have never manifested any brand loyalty to any specific philosophic line. Today the performing philosopher does not come down the mountain with truths carved in stone. He/she comes up to bat several times a day trying to whack out a conceptual hit. In baseball, a batter who gets one hit out of three will usually lead the league.

A thought-inventor is voted into the Hall of Fame or wins the coveted MVP (Most Valuable Philosopher) award on the basis of batting average over the years.

In this book, for example, one-third of the ideas are kinda silly, one-third are kinda boring. But one-third are home runs. When they enter your brains they can inpregnate, fuse with your other thoughts and create new software for programming your life.

Hope you enjoy the game.

PART 1

THE TWILIGHT OF MECHANICAL POLITICS

The Seeds of the 1960s

Spring 1973
San Luis Obispo Prison

These days each decade is a statement in the age-long global human conversation.

In the cultural message of the 1960s every American was, actively or passively, engaged. It so happened that I was most centrally involved in these social changes as member of, and cheer-leader for, a small group of innovative intellectuals who sought to receive, integrate and transmit emerging cultural signals.

The meaning of this explosive decade will be evaluated by history in the light of subsequent developments. It is natural that those who were engaged in the transaction present their versions of what happened and their predictions of the events to come.

In January 1960 I accepted an invitation to come to Harvard University to initiate new programs in what was then called Behavior Change. I was convinced that mental illness could be cured; that drastic limitations on human intellectual and emotional function were caused by inflexible thought-programs imprinted and conditioned neural circuits which created and preserved artificial states of perceived reality and poor mental performance.

I believed the brain to be a bio-chemical-electrical network capable of receiving and creating a changing series of adaptive realities if and when the chemical key for altering consciousness was found and employed in the context of an adequate theory. In the then-zeitgeist of Salk, Fleming, Pauling, I believed that the right chemical used correctly was the cure. The "career ailment" I had selected as curable was human nature.

To oversimplify, I believed that we humans did not know how to program our minds, and that the static, repetitive conditioned software known as the normal mind was itself the source of "dis-ease" and that the task of the

A new science is defined. I have suggested the term Neurologic: the understanding and control of one's own nervous system.

psychologist-neurologoist was to discover the neurochemical for changing mind, i.e., to allow for new imprints of new realities and new conditioned sequences. Our initial experiments at Harvard suggested that L.S.D. might open the brain to reprogramming.

In the early sixties we tested these hypotheses in a series of controlled experiments sharing L.S.D. with several hundred persons under the following conditions: the **set** or expectation was for philosophic exploration and self-discovery; the **setting** was supportive, secure, and respectable. **There was not one casualty or "bad trip."** Our subjects would routinely experience meta-mind intensities and were encouraged to contemplate the personal and social implications of these new signals.

The results of these and other psychedelic drug experiences led us to conclude that organic neuro-chemicals could be used as instruments for studying the nervous system, for freeing brain from the limits of mind, for training human beings to develop new neural circuits (new minds) for reception, integration and transmission.

The implications of these conclusions for human freedom were far-reaching. A new science was defined. I have suggested the term Neurologic: the understanding and control of one's own nervous system. More important, a new mythic conception of human nature emerges. The human being is seen as having many programs (mind operating systems-MOS) which evolve during the course of individual development and which can be turned on and off selectively and adaptably as one "turns on and tunes" the many external electrical circuits surrounding the modern human.

In 1960-63 we tested these theories in a series of objective studies of prison rehabilitation, psychedelic psychotherapy, and personality change. The hypotheses were confirmed. We cut the prison-return rate by 90%. We demonstrated quantitative psychometric improvement in personality. It was prize-winning elegant research. Our subjects shared our enthusiasm but the medical directors didn't. We were naive enough to be surprised that many administrators didn't really want to eliminate the pathologies they administer.

God knows they liked me personally, respected our results and in their secret hearts hoped that we were right. But there is this larval inertial fear of change. Three times I was offered tenure at Harvard (and the post of chief psychologist at Massachusetts General Hospital) if I would just play down the drug research. But by then more than careers were at stake. We had entered the dialogue of myth, tapped into that ancient current of passionate hope and risky belief that humanity can evolve into a higher wisdom. It was the familiar Gnostic,

We were thinking far-out history thoughts at Harvard ... believing that it was a time for visions, knowing that America had run out of philosphy, that a new empirical, tangible meta-physics was needed.

hermetic, Neo-Platonic, alchemical, Faustian, Jeffersonian belief in the individual as microcosm, the all-out vision of multi-centered universe that gives life to individual existence, perennially recurring, always opposed by the Inquisition, always mocked by the current version of authorized dogma.

We were thinking far-out history thoughts at Harvard, some thirty graduate students, young professors and theologians, believing that it was a time (after the shallow, nostalgic fifties) for far-out visions, knowing that America had run out of philosophy, that a new, empirical, tangible cybernetic was desperately needed, knowing in our hearts that the old mechanical myths had died at Hiroshima, the past was over, and politics could not fill the spiritual vacuum.

The vision we offered was the "head-trip"—a scientific, experimental neurologic. Whereas the pre-scientific oriental philosophies and the western mystical off-shoots speak vaguely of the divinity within each person, we tried to operationally redefine the old teachings and to offer an experimental Neo-Platonism. Your brain is the center of your universe. Read any basic text on the nervous system. Learn which of the eight types of drug-yoga turns on which circuits of your nervous system; learn to dial, tune, focus, program and reprogram your brain. Then you learn to accept total responsibility for the realities you construct. (See *Undoing Yourself Too* by Dr. Hyatt).

The basis for this new cybernetic was the belief that advances in modern science now make it possible to develop an understanding of the nervous system, its evolution in the individual and the species, and the effects of chemical and electronic adjuvants on its expanding function. This new understanding of the source and instrument of consciousness is leading us to a truly scientific philosophy of a self-responsible human nature.

The alert and reasonably educated person in 1960 was familiar with the following scientific concepts which, if known by the philosophers of antiquity, would certainly have influenced their theories: (1) The Einsteinian equations concerning relativity and the co-variance of timespace. (2) The nervous system as bio-computer organized in hierarchial centers selectively mediating the reception, storage, analysis and transmission of messages. (3) Elementary computer theory. (4) Electrical and electronic technology providing for selectivity of frequency, intensity and clarity of signal. (5) The D.N.A. code as source of instructions for constructing, maintaining and evolving both body and nervous system.

With these scientific concepts as suggestive text, L.S.D. as navigational tool and prayers for grace, we began to write and to talk publicly about the possibilities of a new philosophy, a new individual cybernetic theology.

All of this educational work was enormously successful. Millions of Americans accepted the "head philosophy," the belief that Ego and "Social Reality" are neural fictions.

At this point (1963) I left Harvard, abandoned the role of conventional, academic scientist and became, a Performing Philosopher. This shift in occupational role was accomplished slowly, hesitantly, exploringly and not without self-conscious humor. First, a diligent study of religious history revealed that psychedelic plants had been used in the great philosophy-generating cultures of the past—Egypt, Persia, India, China and Greece—always for initiation into adulthood, entrance into the spiritual life and for the training of shamans, prophets, and special priests who played colorful and apparently necessary public ceremonial roles. At the same time I began personal training in Hindu Vedanta, Buddhist Tantra, and Taoist techniques for understanding the flow of various energies. The "obligatory pilgrimage" to India occurred.

In 1963 we started centers for training in consciousness expansion, a scientific journal and lecture tours for communicating the results of our research. We were particularly concerned with the development of neurological linguistics, both verbal and, more important, electrical and electronic methods to communicate the broadened range of consciousness.

Our Castalia Foundation in Millbrook, New York was visited by musicians, electronic sound technicians, painters and light technicians. The new modes of art we developed (based on the capacity of the nervous system to receive, synthesize and transmit accelerated, compressed and multi-media presentations) have since been taken over by commercial film and television people. And the computer culture.

All of this educational work was enormously successful. Millions of Americans more or less accepted the "head philosophy," the belief that Ego and "Social Reality" are neural programs, clusters of synaptic connections, consensual paranoias. What might be called a neo-radical-nominalism characterized this philosophic revolution, an invisible, implicit, amused, sometimes pious, detachment from reflex social conventions and the fears they are designed to induce. A general "hip" rejection of partisan politics, war, violence, military service, racism (white and black), enslaved careerism, erotic hypocrisy, sexism, establishment religion, local orthodoxies of dress, grooming, posture, art. A rejection too of pomposity of mind, including one's own, and the platitudinous hippie philosophy itself. This signal of hope and freedom was sent throughout the world. Poets in Soviet prisons heard it. And young people everywhere.

The inevitable backlash from this new message of individual power began in 1966 when various legislatures and Congress began considering bills to criminalize L.S.D. and similar drugs. In this year I testified before two Senate committees urging that control of all mind-changing drugs be assigned to the

History may well decide that the second belligerent disaster of the Johnson administration was the decision to turn drug control over to the police.

medical profession supervised by Federal and State health agencies. I predicted that if control of drugs were administered by law enforcement agencies, the result would be a black market more irrational and widespread than that of alcohol prohibition and the growth of enormous police-state repressive bureaucracy. And who, indeed, wanted that?

This political position then was by no means radical or solitary. Indeed, during the Johnson administration, a bitter battle was fought on this issue. Medical and scientific people (backed by the Kennedys) urged that drugs be administered by the Department of Health, Education and Welfare, while law-and-order people politicked for the Department of Justice. History may well decide that the second great belligerent disaster of the Johnson years was the decision to turn drug control over to the police. L.S.D. was made illegal and most of the top drug scientists began their steady exit from government responsibility. Another war on heresy had been declared.

At this time the "new consciousness" became a political issue indissolubly intertwined with peace, sexual liberation, reform of education, racial equilibrium, ecology, and "end the draft." I suppose the political manifestation was inevitable. So I joined the circuit. Peace, love, and free your head, we said.

It is my folly to believe deeply in the Jeffersonian vision and the First Amendment. I accept this Merlin heritage, this national trust. Could this first America be saved? Well, we said, if they can make laws we can repeal them. With the other dissenting spokesmen I opposed the war and defended marijuana and L.S.D. against unscientific slanders. We warned of the heroin peril and unlicensed, ill-informed drug abuse. I advocated, not drugs (no one had to do that), but a rational, philosophic, scientific understanding of drugs. It was the time (can we remember?) of civil rights, nonviolent dissent debated openly, registered in the polls and litigated in the courts.

I was followed, set-up and busted like everyone else, fought test cases, got the Federal marijuana law declared unconstitutional. It was in the American tradition to defend what you believed. Every court decision and every poll showed that the "new consciousness" was growing. The love-ins, hippie beads, the Beatles and the demonstrations were the silly froth. The real thing had to do with the way people looked each other in the eye and smiled knowing that something new and self-responsible was happening in their heads. The world listened. Messages came to us from the dissenting underground in Russia and Brazil. The real revolution of the sixties was neurological.

The emergence of a new philosophy occurs at rare, crossroads points in history. Political, social, economic changes follow changes in the conceptions of

The seeds of the sixties have taken root underground. The blossoming is to come.

human nature. The consciousness revolution of the sixties initiated what is now called the Information, Communication, Cybernetic Age and challenged all of the institutions and moral principles upon which industrial society was based.

This systematic questioning of the orthodoxies led inevitably to the Nixon counter-reformation, the attempt to re-impose the old authority by means of police power. But the history of Inquisitions teaches that cultural-philosophic matters cannot successfully be legislated despite heresy trials, sumptuary laws, informer-provocateur espionage tactics, and secret police.

A second classic reaction to the collapse of authority is existential loneliness. Once you have accepted that your nervous system creates from the Heraclitan flow your own reality, what guideposts, what compass readings, what new goals? The divergence, individualism, and Utopian optimism of the sixties were crushed by violent reaction. This philosophic vacuum was temporarily filled by a renaissance of old dogmas which latched on to the new energies—evangelical christianity, homogenized Buddhism, TV Hinduism. These pessimistic, nostalgic creeds served to turn-off, shallow-out, calm-down the explosive expansions of the last decade. Jesus Freaks are long-haired rednecks, the Maharishi a CIA agent.

I believe that a new philosophy will be created by those who were born after Hiroshima which will dramatically change the human condition. It will have these characteristics: (1) It will be scientific in essence and science-fiction in style. (2) It will be based on the expansion of consciousness, understanding and control of the nervous system, producing a quantum leap in intellectual efficiency and emotional equilibrium. (3) Politically it will stress individualism, decentralization of authority, a live-and-let-live tolerance of difference, local option and a mind-your-own-business libertarianism. (4) It will continue the trend towards open sexual expression and a more honest, realistic acceptance of both the equality of and the magnetic difference between the sexes. The mythic religious symbol will not be a man on a cross but a man-woman pair united in higher love communion. (5) It will seek revelation and Higher Intelligence not in formal rituals addressed to an anthropomorphic deity, but within natural processes, the nervous system, the genetic code, and without, in attempts to effect extra-planetary communication. (6) It will include practical, technical neurological-psychological procedures for understanding and managing the intimations of union-immortality implicit in the dying process. (7) The emotional tone of the new philosophy will be hedonic, aesthetic, fearless, optimistic, humorous, practical, skeptical, hip. We are now experiencing a quiescent preparatory waiting period. Everyone knows something is going to happen. The seeds of the Sixties have taken root underground. The blossoming is to come.

The Great Judeo-Christian Sin, Outlaw, Guilt, Crime & Punishment T.V. Show

April 1976
Federal Prison, San Diego

"I pulled the gun on the President to call attention to Manson"
— Lynette Fromme

The Average American watches television seven hours a day. This is a neurological fact so ominous in its implications that it cannot be understood in words. Would it take a year of full time Television explanation and neural demonstration for us to understand how our brains have become addicted to electronic "junk," how television creates, manages and schedules our reality, how tonight's crime show becomes next week's crime wave, how the images and illusions of politics are produced?

In order to package and arrange the flow of "news" our television civilization requires a continual supply of newsmakers . . . reality-actors who play parts in the day-time and prime-time shows which define our existence.

And who, besides the "mad-programmer" of ABCBS, understands how news-events are carefully calibrated to meet seasonal scheduling?

It is no accident, for example, that the Wars on Drugs occur in election years, and that political carnivals usually occur as summer replacement shows. They are scheduled to charge up the boredom of summer programming. It's not the heat, it's the cupidity.

Many have wondered why the Watergate investigation was postponed until after the elections of 1972. To avoid prime-time competition! Got It? The Ervin hearings carried us nicely through the desert of summer 1973 and then the scandal cooked along on the back-burners of the evening news until July-August 1974 when the impeachment hearings again filled the programming vacuum. The essence of "news" is, of course, the modern version of Roman coliseum shows and gladiator combats. American civilization, for certain explicit biblical reasons, apparently requires that its leaders, its political heroes be publicly sacrificed.

An enormous industry, similar to the national projects of pyramid-building in Egypt, cathedral-building in medieval Europe, and prison-camp building in

American television culture has added an ancient twist to the familiar "martyr role." In a religious ritual rivaling that of the blood-letting Aztecs, the American people seem to demand the public immolation of top officials, a process called "The Curse of the Oval Room."

Stalinist Russia has emerged in America—the production of political martyrs, fallen heroes and "concept outlaws."

There is nothing new about the political martyr role. In Mammalian politics as in every other competitive game there is a winner and many losers. Martyrs are traditionally produced and exploited by losers to symbolize their resentment against those on top. Dreyfuss, Sacco-Vansetti, the Scottsboro boys, Alger Hiss, Patrice Lumumba, Che Guevara are classic "loser-heroes" all apparently modeled after the guiding sacrifice myth of our epoch—the political assassination of Christ by a gang of Italians.

American television culture has added an ancient twist to the familiar "martyr role." In a religious ritual rivaling that of the blood-letting Aztecs, the American people seem to demand the public immolation of its top officials. This mysterious process has been called "The Curse of the Oval Room" to remind us that, since 1900 (the beginning of American Empire) the psycho-history of the American Presidency reveals an ominous record of failure, break-down and death.

1900—William McKinley	assassinated
1904—Theodore Roosevelt	repudiated in 1912
1908—William Howard Taft	repudiated in 1912
1912—Woodrow Wilson	physical and mental breakdown; repudiated while in office
1920—Warren Harding	died in office
1924—Calvin Coolidge	*
1928—Herbert Hoover	repudiated in 1932
1932—Franklin Roosevelt	died in office
1948—Harry Truman	repudiated while in office
1952—Dwight Eisenhower	**
1960—John F. Kennedy	assassinated
1964—Lyndon Johnson	repudiated while in office
1968—Richard Nixon	repudiated while in office
1972—Gerald Ford	repudiated in 1976
1976—Jimmy Carter	repudiated in 1980
1980—Ronald Reagan	disgraced in 1988

To summarize this wretched record of executive sacrifice: of the last 16 presidents, four have died, ten have been repudiated, and only two, Coolidge and Eisenhower, coasted out of the White House, with any psycho-political

*Alleged to have died before assuming office
**Heart failure while in office

The "outlaw-sin industry" depends on the cooperation of three groups:
  1. The sinners are the talent.
  2. The defense and prosecuting lawyers are the producers.
  3. The media provides the artistic direction.

rapport. Does some sort of mythic mystery operate here? One is reminded of the "Ritual of the Slain Hero" which, in antiquity, demanded the fall of the leader—Dionysus, Anu, Adonis, Attis, Lao, Jesus, Osiris and which in modern times has cursed the American throne of global power.

This ritual destruction of The Leader is a topic which deserves a more detailed analysis. The series of televised ordeals through which candidate-martyrs must pass to reach the sacrificial altar of the Oval Room is particularly awe-inspiring in an election-year. In this more modest essay, however, we shall consider the phenomenon of the "public outlaw or sinner," the enormous media industry which commercializes it, and the omnipotent lawyer-caste which produces it.

The Outlaw Martyrs

> Patty and the Harrises read about Jack Scott's new notoriety in the newspaper room of the Sacramento Public Library where they went to keep acquainted with the media chronology of the SLA saga . . . In their accumulated stacks of books and newspaper clippings they still had the unfinished manuscript Scott had helped them write before their falling out . . . Bill seized upon an idea. They could do Jack and themselves a favor if the manuscript could be sold to a major book publishing company.
>
> In early May an SLA messenger presented the proposal to Scott in San Francisco. If Scott would play literary agent for the fugitives, they would split the profits with him . . . "
>
> —*Rolling Stone*

The "Outlaw-Sin" Industry depends upon the cooperation of three groups:
  1. The sinners are the talent.
  2. The defense and prosecuting lawyers are the producers.
  3. The media provides the artistic direction.

Like the movie and record business the Outlaw-Sin Industry needs a continual supply of new faces and groups.

The more leisurely print-cultures of the past required no more than one "Concept Criminal" a generation. Dreyfuss. Scopes. Alger Hiss. Today's voracious television appetite requires a new crop of outlaws each year. 1975, for example, gave us Joan Little, Hurricane Carter, Donald Cinque De Freeze, Patty, Squeaky, Jane Moore, Emily and Bill Harris, not to mention a return of the irrepressible Berrigan Brothers, the perennial pranks of Dick Gregory and the re-incarnation come-back of Eldridge Cleaver.

Criminals/sinners—from the Black Panthers to FBI chiefs and White House Officials—appear on the scene, make their play, and get dragged off stage, but the lawyers remain administrating and profiting from the action and booking in the next show.

The rituals and performances of "Concept Criminals" are totally stereotyped and perfectly understood by both the players and the consuming public.

1. A symbolic crime publicly committed or exposed.
2. The chase, arrest or surrender.
3. The Grand Jury or Senate hearings.
4. The pre-trial litigation.
5. The trial and verdict.
6. Sale of media rights by the lawyers.

The Symbolic Crime must be committed in the name of a higher cause. The criminal, in violation of the customs of the professional crook, passionately confesses and even claims credit for the deed! The taboo-infraction cannot involve the normal motives—greed or passion. The offense must be a moral flouting of authority. The enormity of the act can range from the sophomoric cutup of the Berrigans to arms, drugs and assassination plots of Ollie North and his criminal gang.

The effect is to morally shock, to incite retaliation, to stir up public opinion. The crime (better described as sin) is directed against a sacred object—the flag, draft-records, an authority figure or symbol—the president, Congress: or it must threaten the sanctified-security—airplane high-jacking, Gordon Liddy's burglary of Democratic headquarters, Black Panther guns in the streets, FBI harassment of pacifists and sanctuary churches.

The Chase is, of course, the most basic mammalian thrill—celebrated in every TV crime show and realized in the hunt for the Weather Underground, the SLA. The smoking gun of Watergate, the Iran Scam money trail.

The Arrest scene is the climax which ends the first act of the Outlaw Play. The obligatory AP photos and TV shots of the hero, surrounded by grim-faced agents, great climax moment of triumph for the police; the first welcomed spiritual wound for the believers of the symbolized cause.

The Grand Jury or Senate Hearings follow the classic New Testament script and offer the martyr's friends their chance to deny the heretic or to stand defiantly before the cameras. This phase in the drama also allows for the entrance of informers, double agents and Judas ambiguities, John Dean, Bud McFarlane.

The Pre-Trial Litigation brings on stage the defense lawyers who circle the victim like quarreling vultures fighting for control of publicity, of the script and of the defense-fund financing. The victim is also offered options of firing and hiring counsel, of demanding self-defense status or of moving side-stage to wait the sacrificial moment to come.

Just as every Hollywood picture is "put together" by producers, who are always in tight control of the enterprise and reap the lion's share of the profits, so is the Outlaw Industry managed by lawyers.

The Trial and Verdict is the climax of the Second Act of the ritual. From Pontius Pilate to Kunstler, Sirica, Senator Inouye, Prosecutor Walsh, the judgement scene is the central ceremony of industrial civilization. The prosecutors relentlessly present the shocked case of the affronted state; the symbol-hero retaliates with Hir denunciation of Caesar or Congress or State Department wimps and presents the alternate heretical morality.

The verdict is usually determined by current moral-market place values. Blacks and radical spokesmen, in the late 70s had strong guilt-credits upon which to draw; and are usually acquitted. Ruchell Magee, the Black San Quentin convict whose picture was flashed around the world holding a gun to the head of a kidnapped judge—could not be convicted!

It is worth noting that the Establishment figures who violate the game-rules and taboos of the political ethic are invariably condemned (although the shame of their fall is usually seen as punishment sufficient to save them from prison). Senator Joe McCarthy, Parnell Thomas, Nixon, Agnew, Hunt, Liddy, J. Edgar Hoover, Mitchell, Colson, Deaver, Nofziger, Ollie North, Adm. McFarlane have all faced the bar of judgement and lash of coliseum scorn for fallen moralists; the million dollar book contracts soon follow.

The Lawyers are the Producers of the "Outlaw" Show

In a civilized society one expects that violations of social rules would be fairly investigated to determine the true fact and that compassionate intelligence would be applied to compensate the injured and to ensure that the conditions which produced the crime were not repeated. It goes without saying that all parties involved are committed to a search for the "T.R.U.T.H." to borrow the words of Judge John Sirica.

The judicial process in the United States is, however, a bitter adversary enterprise. There is little pretense at establishing scientific facts which could determine whether the accused has committed a crime or whether the circumstances mitigated the misdeed. The judicial climate is enthusiastically competitive. Sides are drawn. Strategies contrived. Secrets kept. Distractions and bluffs are employed by clever lawyers.

Let us state the truth simply. Crime in America is a business which is run by (and for the profit of) those who create the law—i.e. the lawyers.

The American government is a government of lawyers. There are more than 200,000 attorneys on government payrolls!

Much domestic opposition to the American government, much anti-social behavior, criminal and political, is master-minded and administrated by lawyers. Criminals—from the CIA Chiefs, to Wall Street traders, to Televangelists

Are we not all media-trained to recognize the nattily dressed man carrying the chic briefcase who flanks the accused?

—appear on the scene, make their play, and get dragged off stage, but the lawyers remain administrating and profiting from the action and booking in the next show. It is conservative to estimate that half of the profits from criminal activities in this country end up in the hands of lawyers. Litigating crime is a multi-billion dollar business controlled by the Power of Attorney.

The old cliche must be up-dated: crime does not pay for the three victims of every crime—the victim, the tax-payer and the crook. Crime does pay, however, and handsomely, for the attorneys who produce the National Crime-Sin Show.

And nowhere is the exploitation of the public, the victims and the criminal more obvious than in the Symbolic Outlaw business.

"This is a terrible thing. I guess the young people don't want to fight anymore," said William Kunstler, after Underground Weatherwoman Jane Alpert surfaced and announced that she was giving up illegal revolutionary activities.

When all is said and done the culminating goal of most radical activism in this country seems to be The Trial. Surely no one with more than two fingers of forehead ever believed that an armed revolution was possible in America. In the last decade the sporadic violence expressed by the New Left was and still is symbolic, "Exemplary actions," to use the jargon of the Weather romantics. Everyone knows that militancy results not in the overthrow of the government but in the well-publicized court trial.

And behind the rhetoric and the headlines operate the Movement Lawyers who encourage, plan, incite, and aid the illegal actions that they later defend in court. Just as every Hollywood picture is "put togther" by producers, who, although less well-known than actors and directors, are always in tight control of the enterprise and reap the lion's share of the profits, so is the Outlaw Industry managed by lawyers.

Let us recall that the prime-time Outlaw capers of the last decade are better remembered by their indictment-label, and numbers. The Chicago Seven. What was their crime? Who were they? The New York 21. The Hunt-Liddy Watergate Gang. What did they do? We recall the cases of Huey Newton and Angela Davis and Bobby Seale and Lyn Nofziger but are vague about the specific acts they were accused of. It is the memory of dissident courtroom postures and legal defenses that remains.

Which brings us to the box-office issue of the Outlaw Business: Defense Funds. Eldridge Cleaver, in 1976, muses that over a million dollars were raised for the Huey Newton trials. Where did the money go? The Ellsberg-Russo trial cost $800,000. How? Why? Where did the money go?

The American media-consumer is judge-jury-parlor-dictator choosing at whim and with a flick of the dial, the winner and losers in the consumer competition.

The scenario is stereotyped. Four times I have found myself in jail-visiting rooms shortly after the bust talking to the lawyers. The first item of business is the Defense Fund. Planning the benefits, the mailing list appeals, the fund-raising cocktail parties.

The routine defense of defense funds goes like this: the government has endless resources to hire prosecutors, investigators, experts, to pay for tests, transcripts and deposition interviews. Should not the political martyr be entitled to the same army of professional bureaucrats? What injustice! Surely ideological criminals such as Ollie North should have as much money to spend on lawyers as the government!

The Symbolic Criminals themselves do not question the process. What choice is there for the sinner-outlaws facing possible imprisonment? Looking for forum justification? Reassured by the proffered support? And they do know the script.

The rewards for the producer-barrister are not limited to financial. Aphrodisiac fame beckons to the defender of the conceptual defendant. Are we not all media-trained to recognize the nattily dressed man carrying the chic briefcase who flanks the accused? His denunciations of injustice quoted in the morning paper. Applaud, please, this courageous fighter for the cause, flamboyantly risking a contempt-of-court citation.

The most successful of the Movement lawyers is William Kunstler, who stole the show in the Joan Little trial (1976) with a swift media maneuver that merits text-book consideration. In one day Battling Bill flew to Raleigh, North Carolina, walked into the on-going trial of a black woman, presented himself to the judge as a consultant counsel, was rejected by the court as unnecessary, received a contempt citation for his fiery denunciation, was sentenced to **two hours** incarceration (!), held a press conference after release, and took the late afternoon flight back north! The network news that night featured the bold Crusader raid. Bravo Bill! (Joan Little spent the night, as usual, in her jail cell.) At the present time Kunstler is stlil flying around the country offering his services to symbolic criminals whose cases promise wire-service appeal. (Joan Little is now in the state prison serving a seven-to-ten-year sentence.)

In fairness to the attorneys it should be pointed out that their production-monopoly on the Crime Business is not their central interest. Let us give credit where credit is due. Lawyers run the government, they run the corporations and they run the labor unions.

The Mass Media Direct The Crime Show

So far we have discussed how the Outlaw Industry operates without asking the more basic question: Why? Fame and fortune are, of course, the goals of the

Today, reality is created mainly by television and movies. The media producers have become a priest-caste who guide, direct, and manage reality.

actors, producers, directors. But why do the consumers buy the stereotyped act?

The first answer: entertainment. "The News" is Spectacle, Manufactured Drama, Diversion from Boredom, the chance to vicariously live a richer life. The American media-consumer is judge-jury-parlor-dictator—choosing at whim and with a flick of the dial, the winner and losers in the consumer competition.

Transgressors—both mercenary and conceptual—play a key role in the religious rituals of an electronic media culture. Crooks commit crimes. Conceptual outlaws commit sins. The ceremonies of hunting sinners, publicly trying them, and assigning retribution is the **basic religious ceremony** of our Moralistic Calvinist Culture.

Let's face it, the conceptual outlaws—Patty Hearst, Lt. Calley, North, Liddy, Berrigan, Huey Newton—although tried in criminal courts—are clearly media-heretics, taboo-witch-craft, Inquisition, **persecution for belief.**

At an even deeper level the Outlaw industry plays an important role in the genetics of the species. Human evolution, we have learned recently, is the evolution of the nervous system, the metamorphic growth in contelligence (consciousness-intelligence) as new circuits of the brain emerge. The civilized primate possesses a four-brain nervous system—bio-survival, motion-emotion, symbolic and social. The key factor in neural evolution is communication. The more evolved the species, the faster, the more complex and the more flexible the modes of communication.

Reality is defined for each species by its channels and methods of communication. A primitive tribe communicates by means of grunts, gestures, jungle drums, runners, smoke-signals. The early species of domesticated primates communicated in terms of printed pages, pictures, costumes, religious dramas, songs and statues. The reality thus created preserved social morality and the social survival techniques which guide the pre-electronic species.

Today, reality is created mainly by television and movies. The media producers have become a priest-caste who guide, direct, and manage reality.

"I ain't gonna work on Maggie's farm no more . . ."

"Don't follow leaders! Watch your parking meters!"

When Bob Dylan sang these lines in the 1960s, he was performing philosophy, transmitting powerful new ideas for which his mass audience was ready. Dylan thus triggered off heretical, sinful acts of resistance to authority, rejection of militarism, refusal to join the mechanical factory culture.

The Establishment Press is a powerful genetic tool in defining and defending the domesticated ethic. The news is "managed" in a cybernetic feed-back loop in which the press tells the public exactly what it senses the public wants to be told

The game is fierce and merciless. Almost everything is tolerated if kept private. One public slip, one show of vulnerability and the fatal image is fixed. SHOT: MUSKIE weeping in snow of New Hampshire lost him the presidency. CUT TO: Gary Hart on "Monkey Business" with Bimbo on lap

so the public will buy the paper. Headlines, emphasis, spinning and twisting stories, slants and plants, photos are all part of the image shaping, and define the actors who personalize the morality drama. The game is fierce and merciless. While almost everything is tolerated if kept private, one public slip, one show of vulnerability and the image is fixed. SHOT: Muskie weeping in the snow of New Hampshire. CUT TO: Wallace standing at the schoolroom door. FLASH: Gary Hart on the "Monkey Business" with the Bimbo on his lap.

"Public Image" is a collective neurological imprint which requires continual reenforcement. Just as the private citizen must be reminded every minute of his waking life that he is who he thinks he is—so must public image be maintained by means of repetition. The persona of Winston Churchill, for example, had to be hammered out like a metallic mask and once formed had to be continually worked on to keep the features clear. One false move—and the mask is badly damaged, perhaps irreparably.

An amusing twist in media-image-making occurred in the Patty Hearst case. For a century the Hearst empire has probably been responsible for more lurid-pop caricature media images than any other reality-industry in the land. And suddenly it became necessary for Hearst's San Francisco *Examiner* to change the image of America's most famous terrorist into the role of a misguided innocent girl. And a tearful Mrs. Hearst denounces the press for pre-judging **her** child!

Television, is of course, the major manufacturer and seller of the Ideological Crime Show. We are familiar with the classic TV confrontations: cowboys-Indians, cops and robbers, Zionists and Palestinians, short-hairs versus hippies, FBI vs. terrorists. Six months after SWAT premiers on prime-time, imitation SWAT teams of kooky-cops are organized in every local police force and a new vigilante tactic is popularized. Angry husbands who, a year ago would have smashed a dish on the floor and headed for the neighborhood saloon, now obediently grab a gun, hold the Missus hostage and docilely crouch in the parlor until TV crews arrive and bull-horns command them to come out with their hands on their heads.

By 1987 the American appetite for the exposure and public trial of conceptual criminals and charismatic sinners had become insatiable. This bumper year gave us, among the Sexy Charismatics— Gary Hart, Ollie North, Jim and Tammy Bakker, Jimmy Swaggart. The youthful sexual and G.I. Joe misdemons of Rev. Pat Robinson were briefly exposed. And, even our greatest charismaster, Ronald Reagan, had his televised moments of Iranscam doubt and shame ("mistakes were made"). Quickly pardoned by the majority of viewing Americans.

The word "charisma" is important in any discussion of neuropolitics. It is defined as "1. A rare or exceptional ability for motivating large numbers of people. 2. A divinely inspired gift or psychological power to incite sudden, unexpected (miraculous?) change in human behavior."

Among the Stern Fundamentalists who were caught in transgressions were Judge Ginsberg, Joseph Biden, Paul Deaver, Lyn Nofziger, Admirals MacFarlane and Poindexter. (Unlike the Cute Charismatics, Stern Funcamentalists are never involved in sex scandals. Their sins usually involve lying, wheeling and dealing.)

Notice how the line between "reality" and electronic fabrication has become blurred. The brilliant performance of Ollie North made him an instant TV star. Luscious Fawn Hall is signed up by the William Morris Agency. Ollie resigns and is inundated by lavish offers to lecture. Judge Bork, after his humiliation, quits the bench to hit the talk show circuit. The week he is convicted of felonious corruption, Paul Deaver goes on a PR tour to hype his just-published book.

Political criminals quickly lose their power when they fall from the White House. Their book-length apologies are scanned for bits of scandal-gossip and then they disappear. John Mitchell? John Dean? Spiro Agnew? Don Regan? Why did they leave us?

Why? Because they were by-the-book-law-and-order bureaucrats who lack charm and charisma.

The only political felon to maintain a celebrity status after his disgrace was your brash friend and mine, G. Gordon Liddy. Twenty years after his bungled burglary at Watergate Gordon ends up as a talk-show host and featured player in **Miami Vice.**

Why? Because G. Gordon is a show-off. He has a certain spunky, swagger and comic wit. Liddy does not have charisma.

Charisma

The word charisma, is important in any discussion of Neuropolitics.

Charisma is defined as: "1. A rare quality or communication skill attributed to those persons who demonstrate an exceptional ability for motivating large numbers of people. 2. A divinely inspired gift or self-taught psychological power to incite unexpected, sudden (miraculous?) change in human behavior."

This discussion of charisma brings us to the cases of TV evangelists who get caught in highly publicized sin. The scenario here is quite different from the White House criminals. The charismatic guys gain fame by claiming to possess a "divinely inspired gift." Their sin is not that they have become secretly wealthy. The Calvinist dogma teaches that the agents of the King of Kings and Lord of Lords should be prosperous and inhabit mansions.

The Charismatic Evangelist's fall is due to sex. Kinky sex. It is attributed to the innate sinfulness of man, the evil powers of promiscuous women and the cunning of the devil whose wicked agents are often found impersonating

The charismatic, self-appointed Voice of God appears on the television screen skillfully producing an altered state of consciousness, seducing the audience into classic voodoo trances. Inciting in hypnotized brains fierce religious-tribal fanaticism.

trollops in sleazy motels. The Jim Bakkers and Swaggarts are tried by their congregations. They confess on screen. They weep. They beg for the blood of Jesus to wash away their sins and infections. Because they claim divine power they receive the ultimate punishment. They are condemned to the lowest level of Hell. They lose their profitable Tourist Lands, their enormous salaries, their mansions and—the final lash—their access to the electronic equipment through which they transmit their contagious ideas.

The Electronic Ministry

The sudden emergence of television evangelism is a fascinating aspect of electronic technology tapping into the most powerful human motivations. The charismatic, self-appointed Voice of God appears on the television screen skillfully producing an altered state of consciousness, passionately seducing the audience into classic voodoo trances. Inciting in hypnotized brains fierce religious-tribal fanaticism.

Take the Pat Robertson "700 Club" as example.

For starters, the show's production is state-of-the-art prime-time TV. It uses the same slick mesmerizing techniques that entrance us into buying Coors Beer and extra-strength Tylenol. The actors on the show look like local news anchors. Dignified Ben Kinchlow with his white trimmed mustache looks like a Supreme Court justice. When the lovely assistant, Danuta Soderman, makes the pitch for money, she looks like a model for some sensible home product as Drano or Roach Motel.

The program builds efficiently towards its climax. Buckle your seat belt, trippers, while shaman Pat leans over, his eyes clenched, his face grimacing in that look of painful sincerity. Hey, the guy is dialing up God, the big sponsor in the sky! The Lord is talking to him! Shirley MacLaine calls it channeling. But for Pat it's more serious. The King of Kings is communicating his impatience with what's happening down here in God's country. Almighty Lord, sitting on his heavenly throne is "sick and tired" (Reagan's favorite phrase) at America being taken over by sinners, homosexuals, Democrats, liberals, secular humanists, atheistic scientists, communist dupes, pornographers. And for some reason (see Revelations) God has a special-hard on for Iranians.

Meanwhile, the pious looking Ben is softly sighing, beseeching, moaning, "Jesus! Jesus!"

Then Pat starts begging the Vengeful Lord to strengthen and arm his people to deal with his enemies. Tension builds. Pat and Ben get a voodoo rhythm going. Then the camera zooms in for close-ups of the audience, holding hands, faces twisted with abdominal pain, softly chanting the name of the Lord.

Tell me about peaceful, smiling group trance-possession sessions, chum. Hey! I've been to a "Grateful Dead" concert! No painful expressions there abouts.

As I watched this show with amazement I suddenly realized what's happening here. These bozos are all high as kites! They're participating in a full-blown shamanic, psychedelic voodoo-possession ceremony.

Listen. I know how these events develop. As part of my professional duties I've participated in about as many group trance experiences as the next guy. William S. Burroughs and Brian Gysen took us up to the Rif mountains of Morocco to this village of shepherd-musicians who have been practicing for 3000 years the oldest religion known. The pagan worship of nature. The rites of Pan-Dionysius. They sit around emitting a serene, peaceful contentment and smoke Moroccan cigarettes and people drum and chant and then, one by one they perform the possession ritual, each dancing out the rhythms of a recognizable divinity—the animal god, the sexual god, the wise old man god, the bisexual god. There's a certain divine humor here as they clown-mimic the clumsy gestures of the Christian rituals. Throughout everyone smiles and beams contentment.

Ted Markland and one of the "Easy Rider" stars took us to the Navaho peyote version of the 700 club on the Arizona desert where the sky is ebony velvet matte and the stars flash like the laser show at a Pink Floyd concert and we sat around watching the exquisitely sculptured fire, listening to drums and chants. And then someone picks up the rattle/feather tele-phone and starts passing on the confident life-affirming message of the particular G.O.D. (God On Duty) at the moment, or the Divine Spirit who happened to pick up the phone. Then the rattle-feather is passed and the next person dials up a long-distance conversation with another G.O.D. All through the night everyone feels calm, grateful, friendly.

Tell me about peaceful, smiling group trance possession sessions, chum. Hey! I've been to a "Grateful Dead" concert! No painful expressions there abouts.

I've channeled with Hassidic rabbis in the ashram garden at dawn when they strapped leather around my arm and we *davined* up the phone numbers of a lot of G.O.D.s. None of them judgmental or vengeful, by the way, Pat.

Have you engaged in those Hindu funereal rites where these guys hand around burning human bodies, sacred wood and ganga on the banks of the Ganges? If so, then you recall that same serene empathic mood.

For me, the most sophisticated and powerful possession rites are the voodoo. Again the hypnogogic group ritual, the drums and songs the smoke and then some participant is possessed by a G.O.D. The human is called the horse who is ridden by the divinity called loa. "It takes a strong horse to carry a big loa." Read

Now fun is fun, Pat. But there are certain rules to the game of god-play.

Michael Ventura's masterful book *Dancing in the USA* (Tarcher), for a moving, scholarly treatment of this African-pagan phenomenon. So. Swear me in, bailiff, and I'll testify as an expert witness that the born again rites of our home-grown southern evangelicals are authentic group-possession trips and that Pat Robertson and Jimmy Swaggart perform the classic shamanistic role of charismatic brain-washing, mind-possession.

At the moment when the ROM of their followers is opened up, they RAM in their sacred software program that is called the Bible. No question, it works. The Biblical meme (paradigm) takes over the brain. They are born-again, i.e. their bio-computers are re-programmed.

Now fun is fun, Pat. But there are certain rules to the game of god-play.

1: if the message you get motivates you to some frenzied, zealous action on the material plane, you're not connected to a G.O.D. You've booted up some primitive software program that some human laid on you. Probably with the best intentions.

2: if any appeals for money or political support are implied, you've obviously dialed the branch office of some commercial or local political organization. Operators on duty 24 hours to receive your contributions.

3: if the possession ritual connects you with some invisible intelligence that claims He is the one and only G.O.D. and that "He will have no other G.O.D.s before Him"? And if he claims that His software program (the Bible) is the complete gospel? And that all those who do not submit are agents of the Devil?

Well, there goes the neighborhood!

Pat Robertson, no question about it. You can summon up the transcendental power. But you break all the rules of the neuro-genetic game when you claim that there is only one form to the universe. At your service to cure hemorrhoids, divert hurricanes and become leader of the Republican Party.

Jimmy Swaggart, even your loyal cousin Jerry Lee Lewis knows that you're out of tune when you claim that this eternal and unchangeable 4.5 billion year old super-intelligence, has, amazingly enough, selected you to be His Spokesman and the business manager of the profitable monopoly involved.

As I watched Robertson incite hatred of non-believers, I was reminded of those familiar TV news scenes in which mobs in the streets of Teheran lash themselves with chains into frenzies of sorrowful rage against Sunni Moslems, Iraquis, Christians, and other agents of the Great Satan.

Discounting stylistic cultural differences, there do seem to be striking similarities between our charismatic evangelicals and the ayatollah. They're both media shamen, charismatic wizards who use television to change people's behavior.

Partners In Time

September 1973
Folsom Prison

A letter came to me in Folsom Prison from Vienna transmitting a friendly signal from Andrei Amalrik and his beautiful wife. Andrei is serving his second three-year sentence in a Russian prison for predicting the decline and fall of the Soviet state. The KGB plans to keep him incarcerated for life.

Vasilios Choulos, Kent Russell and Melvin Belli have just written a brief challenging my illegal kidnapping in Afghanistan by American agents. We sent a copy to Kim Dae Jung, who was abducted from Japan by South Korean agents. The American government protested the illegal snatching of Kim because the secret leaked.

Alexandros Panagoulis, just released from five years in Greek prison, is broadcasting his message of intransigent courage. He's going to write a book, if they let him. The secret police hate publicity.

Meanwhile, Alexander Solzhenitsyn, novelist, and Andrei Sakharov, physicist, continue to uncover facts about Soviet police methods:

> But here we have a peculiarity, I would almost say an advantage of our social structure: not a single hair falls or will fall from my head or from the heads of members of my family without the knowledge or approval of the KGB. That is the extent to which we are observed, shadowed, spied upon and listened to.

Nixon in the White House. Brezhnev rules the U.S.S.R. Maoism terrorizes China.

And just in the background underground waiting for *glasnost* are millions of dissident Russians, libertarian Chinese and cybernetic Americans.

Here, in 1973, we watch the great factory powers writhe through the last hours of the industrial age. Breznev rules the USSR, Maoism terrorizes China. Nixon connives in the White House.

Meanwhile, just below the horizon, a new model of human is emerging. The mechanical-productive conformist of the factory civilization is losing status and is being replaced by the open, losened up individuality required of the information society.

By the year 1998 two-thirds of the members of the U.S. House of Representatives will have been, thirty years before, fans of Bob Dylan and the Beatles.

Millions of young Soviet intellectuals read western magazines, watch blackmarket video tapes, listen to rock 'n' roll, communicate in *samizats*, swap anti-authority jokes—waiting restlessly for *glasnost*. Young educated Chinese, especially in the arts and sciences, reject the robot model and follow western culture enviously. South Korean students watch American TV on the U.S. Armed Forces networks and ready themselves to hit the streets.

As our species lurches nervouly into the information age, every industrial country adjusts to the new cultural values. A cybernetic society demands instant, free flow of information. The post-war generation in every industrial power is beginning to recognize its strength and its obligation.

By the year 1998 two-thirds of the members of the U.S. House of Representatives will have been, thirty years before, fans of Bob Dylan and the Beatles.

And, amazingly enough, their age-counterparts in China, USSR, South Korea will have picked up the beat.

Political Voyeurism

September 1973
Folsom Prison

The compulsion to spy on others is derived, so it is said, from the sexual curiosity of the pre-pubescent child who burns to know what grown-ups do behind bedroom doors. Reaching maturity the sexually confident person expresses erotic energy in lovemaking. The voyeurism of childhood remains as a delicious form of foreplay. For those who do not mature sexually, whose erotic expressions are inhibited, voyeurism, the surreptitious spying on others, can become a highly sexual obsession. As with most other guilt-ridden "sexual deviates," the voyeur is invariably a political conservative—shocked, moralistic, and censorious about behaviors which he compulsively and secretly seeks to discover. We think of the priest in the confessional or of vice squads or of J. Edgar Hoover, forbidding extramarital expressions to his agents on pain of discharge, and who, himself unmarried, presumptive virgin *voyeur extraordinaire*, guarded files containing reports, tapes, and photos of the sexual peccadillos of American politicians.

We define the 1960s as a time of erotic explosion. But the freedom of sexual expression was not shared by all. While part of the population was making love, another part was reading spy novels about enemies doing bad things that must be investigated and stopped. The cold war petered out when it became obvious that the Commie leaders were basically hard-working, no-nonsense law and order folk and that the "bad" things were being done right here in America by grass-smoking, long-haired people who were growing in numbers and influence.

So the C.I.A. is called home to join the Hoover-gang and the Liddy-plumbers in spying on their fellow Americans.

Gordon Liddy Auditions
For Miami Vice North

August 1973
Folsom Prison

It was Saturday night—the 64-room mansion at Millbrook, New York, filled with staff members of the Castalia Foundation and weekend guests. Dinner in the oak-paneled dining room, low tables and cushions. The big stereo speakers trembled with Dylan, Beatles, Ali Akbar. Later, around the huge fireplace, Jimi played guitar. Musicians came to Millbrook to learn that sound was energy to play with. Strange new vibrations filled the air. Painters, discovering that light was energy to free from canvas, splashed, rippled, exploded color across the walls of Millbrook, chromatic patterns bubbling, rainbow crystals blossoming, multi-hued cellular blobs undulating. Beautiful women moved with yogic grace and most of the men wore longish hair. The year was 1965.

Outside the house, crouched behind dark bushes, binoculars glued to his eyes, G. Gordon Liddy peered through the windows at the activities within the mansion. He, the first "square" American to witness a "psychedelic" light show, was whispering instructions to the walkie-talkie pressed tenderly against his cheek. Twenty uniformed, booted, armed sheriffs in cowboy hats were staked out around the mansion, a real-life T.V. posse led by two assistant D.A.'s, Alphonse Rosenblatt and G. Gordon Liddy. It was decided to wait until the revelers within the castle retired to their bedrooms. Liddy was used to waiting. Castalia had been under surveillance for weeks. G. Gordon Liddy and commando staff hidden behind trees, noting who slept where. And then, back in the courthouse, endless conferences with maps, floor plans, schedules. It was an exciting prime-time caper. Miami Vice North!

At midnight the raiders burst into the mansion, pushing open unlocked doors. Liddy leading four troopers bounded upstairs to the third floor and smashed open the door to the master bedroom. She was reclining on pillows on the mirror bed. I was sitting on the edge of the bed talking to my son Jack and his friend. I stood up and looked into the wild eyes of G. Gordon Liddy.

The "big raid on Millbrook" was a bungled bust. No evidence found. But Liddy, undaunted raced around the country talking breathlessly to astonished Rotarians about his crusade against sin.

We were ordered, illegally, "Don't move," while nervous deputies searched the room, confiscating Her innocent geranium plants and boxes of papers. I was given permission to call a lawyer, but mysteriously, the phone was "out of order." Rosenblatt and Liddy took me aside to a small, unused bedroom and played out the Mutt-Jeff, good-guy-bad-guy interrogation. Many policemen are ham actors and love to initiate deep conversations. In their hearts they cherish envy and a secret hope that the sinner will get away with it.

As I have done a thousand times, I patiently outlined the scientific, philosophic, historical, political and legal dimensions of what we were doing. Rosenblatt argued gently. Gordon scolded me about narcotics, addiction, the murder-weed, moral corruption, and running us out of the county. That's a tape I'd like to have played back.

I recall one zany moment. Gordon accused us of being dangerous enemies of society. I explained that some society, somewhere, someday, would be very grateful for what we were doing. Then Liddy made this strange, enigmatic, theological prediction. "Hell will freeze over," he said, "before the people of this county erect a statue of you in the town square."

The "big raid on Millbrook" was, of course, a bungled bust, the search warrant illegal, no evidence found, the case thrown out of court. But Liddy, undaunted, raced around the country talking breathlessly to wide-eyed Rotarians about his crusade against wickedness. He used the first-initial middle-name label in imitation of his hero, J. Edgar Hoover, G. Gordon Liddy.

American Military Helicopters
Buzz Our Cybernetic Teepees

July 1973
Folsom Prison

Well, this cops and robbers drama which was to last so long and involve such a global cast of characters had just begun. The surveillance seige of Castalia continued. Roadblocks. Automatic stop-and-search of every long-haired car. Strange looking men were coming around to repair the phone once a week. I felt secure. Circuit One scanning revealed that no one was going to be killed. Circuit Two instincts assured that we had control of the territory. We allowed no illegal drugs in the house. There must be a hundred stashes still buried in the woods for future archeologists to uncover. Minor possession beefs were nothing to worry about. No one went to jail for a handful of grass. It was comforting to know that the townspeople of Millbrook were with us. By this time the locals knew us well. We were the best customers of every store in town. The thirty people at Castalia spent one hundred thousand dollars a year in a tiny town with a two-block shopping district. Our people were young, good-looking, happy, open. The conservative village naturally adopted and protected us against the ambitious, tricky politicians from Poughkeepsie. Millbrook was populated by tradesmen and workers whose families had settled there to service the castle where we lived. Dietrich, the utilities baron who created the estate, had made his money in carbide lighting. He was the first to popularize the new form of illumination. Legend whispered that every street light in the state of New York was testimony to his genius. He imported hundreds of Italian stonemasons to build gates, towers, bridges, miles of stone walls, a Bavarian bowling alley, waterfalls, gothic garden cottages. For thirty years after his death the grand estate had

**Then we swept in with young Mellon wealth and Harvard charisma.
The lawns were lush and green again. The great castle gleamed with light.**

crumbled in disuse. Wild vegetation covered the lawns and gardens. The
nobility drained away. Rich Americans lacked the energy to maintain estates
with acres of lawns and gardens.

Then we swept in with young Mellon wealth and Harvard charisma. The
lawns were lush and green again. The great castle gleamed with light. Young
people rich with confidence and vision drove through the huge portcullis gates,
a new aristocracy. (Aside from the cosmic God satori business, what acid did to
millions of young people was to *ennoble* them, crack them loose from the middle
class monolith, free them to wander around the country, a new amateur royalty
playing in the garden of incredible goodies, treating the world as a here-now
paradise to be gratefully enjoyed. The Laguna Beach hippies used to dance
barefoot through the beaches and mountains murmuring, "Thank you God.")

The village of Millbrook stirred again with grandeur, however funky and
controversial. World attention focused on the castle grounds. Once again the
village watched and listened and gossiped about the goings-on at the Big House.
And once again the Grand Old Party politicians from Poughkeepsie stirred with
know-nothing, Cromwellian puritan anger at anything "foreign," glamorous,
frivolous, elegant. One of the many curious aspects of American culture is the
absence of an "upper" class, a "high" society, an hedonic aristocracy. America
since Lincoln has been a heavy, feet-on-the-ground John Wayne society. The
triumph of mediocrity and practicality. America has just reached that stage of
growth when military, political, and economic security makes possible the
emergence of an erotic Psi-Phy philosophic elite. The alchemical renewal. The
time trip. Alexandria. Eleusis. Delhi under the Moguls. Elizabethan England.
Palermo. Prague. **Konorak** and **Khajuraho**. The India of King Asoka. The Chou
Dynasty in China.

At the Millbrook summer pageants a hundred consciously garbed pagans
wandered through the grounds, under wide porticos. Ambassadors came from
the cultural duchies, from Herman-on-Hudson, from RAND, from Palo Alto,
from Hyannisport, from Bethesda, from Beverly Hills. From "high" society
came Ronnie Laing, Allen Ginsberg, Alan Watts, Ken Kesey, swamis, gurus,
stars of every magnitude, while great musicians strolled across terraces filling
the warm air with sound, light machines poured color patterns on the outside
walls, fountains played.

And, in the bushes, his Fordham morals outraged, his soviet mind seething
with civil service ambitions, G. Gordon Liddy watched.

Twice a week we would hear the ominous flap-flap-flap of the whirling paddles and watch the sheriff's helicopter circling above and men with cameras and binoculars pointed at Arcadian bliss.

The roadblocks and surveillance continued, so we closed the castle and set up camps in the forests. The teepee is the most sensual living arrangement ever designed by humanity; soft, fur-lined nosecone of pleasure pointed at the stars.

Twice a week we would hear the ominous flap-flap-flap of the whirling paddles and watch the sheriff's helicopter circling above and men with cameras and binoculars pointed at Arcadian bliss. Liddy used to tell lurid stories of seeing *naked women* (!) emerging from teepees. "The panties are droppping faster than the acid at Leary's Lair" Gordon blurted to the Poughkeepsie paper. This is what police work is all about! We treasured those moments of surveillance, feeling a strong bond of affiliation with Vietnamese peasants and Che Guerillas and African lions and all wild, free creatures on this planet gazing up in surprise at armed agents, Sci-Fi spies in government motor ships. Some of the forest people wondered if we could bring down a helicopter with the power of thought. Others suggested laser rays. But the wheel of karma was to balance everything. G. Gordon Liddy, amazingly enough, was the agent to bring down the Nixon regime!

Woodstock and Watergate

July 1973
Folsom Prison

Head-high dissident youth ended the Vietnam war, drove Johnson from the White House, and would have elevated Robert Kennedy to the presidency, but Sirhan's steel ballots elected Nixon.

If Bobby Kennedy had lived . . . well, among other things, the control of drugs would have been given to physicians and researchers in H.E.W.

The night of his election Nixon was interviewed in the locker room and, in flush of super-bowl victory, revealed the philosophy which was to guide his administration: Keep Fighting. The influence of Vince Lombardi (win at any cost) on the American right-wing cannot be overestimated. It is no accident that Lombardi died in Washington. Another omen.

Nixon was later to blame Watergate on the counter-culture, claiming that his special police force was necessary to deal with anarchy and disorder in the late sixties.

Very few Americans, even in these post-Watergate days, understand how Nixon set up his very own Special Service elite police, whose mission was to harass, intimidate, arrest and imprison dissenters. Under the guise of "drug control" this Orwellian coup was accomplished with the approval of middle-aged liberals. It was so simple. The Narc budget jumped from 22 million to 140 million. Narcs are "mood-police," "thought-police" pursuing the victimless crime of cultural dissent. Constitutional rights were suspended and martial law (no-knock, stop-and-frisk, curfew, etc.) was imposed selectively on one easily identifiable segment of the population, the victims exactly those who are persecuted by the same police tactics in communist, socialist, and right-wing dictatorships throughout the world. Nixon nixing pant-suits and Agnew rock and roll.

Fear descended upon this land. The spokesmen for the counter-culture were arrested, harassed, silenced. The press cooperated completely, endorsed the dope-pogram and piously denounced the counter-cultures.

Fear descended upon this land. The spokesmen for the counter-culture were arrested, harassed, silenced. The press cooperated completely. Slanting reporters, columnists, and editorial writers endorsed the dope-pogram and piously denounced the counter-culture. Most everyone born before 1930 hated the sixties, felt alienated, left behind.

We were told to blame ourselves for being too innocent, optimistic, for failing to recognize the reality of evil. The Manson-Nixon paradox. *Lampoon* editors got rich entertaining *New Yorker* audiences with the bizarre notion that Woodstock was a lemming-assemblage of death-cultists.

Everyone with a media hook, a money itch, an ambition habit can make it by playing on the mediocracy's fear of the free unknown. G. Gordon Liddy, on the basis of his Millbrook dramatics, rides it to the White House as super-narc. Any ex-Marine with a sadism kink too conspiratorial for the F.B.I. or state police volunteers for the new gestapo. American narcs make expense-paid tours around the world teaching foreign police how to detect the new enemy. And at home neo-Puritanism becomes the philosophic cop-out. Cynical retreat from hopeful Utopianism. Swami turn-off passivity. Think little. "Lay low" replaces "stay high."

During the Reagan Reaction Yuppies are so frightened that they line up around the block to work for Maggie's Pa once more. "He hands you a nickel, he hands you a dime, and asks with a Marine-Corps grin, 'Are ya havin' a good time?'" The hottest commercial jingle becomes: "Be ... all that you can be ... in the Aaaaaaarm ... meeeey!

The Adversary Process

June 1973
Folsom Prison

Nixon often referred to "the other side" in justifying his repressive moves. The enemy is whomever keeps one from power. Brezhnev and Mao become allies, useful in keeping one another in office. Villagers bombed in Cambodia are not enemies. They aren't even people. The real enemies of the Republican regimes of Nixon and Reagan are liberals, Democrats, secular humanists, feminists, and the ungrateful minorities and the dissenting young.

This is the global trend that leads to international *detente* and domestic repression. Brezhnev drinks champagne with Nixon and goes home to imprison the Russian dissenters. Algeria patches up its quarrel with America and turns the police on its college students. Nixon swaps oil for jets with the Shah while Iranian students picket in the streets. Etc.

Watergate is the last phase of the War Between the Generations. Nixon, forced to organize special police to deal with protesting youth, picks out his own "good kid" John Dean to be the fall guy. It turns out that Watergate was just a bunch of irresponsible kids masterminded by Dean and Segretti in over-zealous opposition to another bunch of irresponsible kids led by Dan Ellsberg and Tony Russo.

One of the many enlightening facets of Watergate is the growing realization that the whole mess has been created by lawyers. By the "whole mess" I refer to the government. A country run by law is a country ruined by lawyers. It is neurologically impossible for a lawyer or a military man to think creatively or to act in harmony with nature. Obfuscation and opposition based on paralyzed precedent. There are over 200,000 lawyers working for the United States government.

Secrecy & Disinformation are Suicidal Political Tactics in a Cybernetic Society

May 1973
Folsom Prison

If you program your brain with simple-minded polarities, whatever you think comes true and so does its opposite. In his State of the Union message on crime, Nixon vows, "We shall have no pity on criminals." Eight months later he and Agnew are looking around for permissive judges. The adversary process gets everyone in the end. Every jury is hung. Vice versus. We get to play every part in the dramas we initiate. There's no way to avoid total responsibility. The very moment World War II ends, the wheel flips over and the Germans start becoming Americans, Americans transform into good Germans, and the Jews develop the most efficient military and secret police in the world. Beware of your enemies because you are going to become them. Right-wing anti-communists ape Soviet methods. Stalin becomes Czar. "We'll throw every crook in jail," promises John Mitchell. Every prisoner is a jailer. Eldridge taught us that. Roosevelt the great liberator condemns the working man to Archie Bunker slavery. No amnesty, said Nixon. No one learns. A convict leans on my cell bars delightedly cursing Nixon and Agnew. The warden's wife has just been shot. "Those dick-sucking motherfuckers will change their mind about capital punishment now." "How about amnesty for everyone," I suggest, motioning towards him and myself and them over there. "String 'em all up," says the convict who opposes the death penalty.

When you think about it, secrecy is the cause of the whole flap. Ellsberg and Russo published some secrets. Leaks in the White House. The plumbers steal Ellsberg's psychiatric secrets. And bug the Democrat's phone calls. The entire White House is involved in cover-up. The hearings center on cover-up of the cover-up.

I can tell you bugging is nothing to worry about. I've been tapped, surveilled, tailed for ten years. The Algerians knew every move we made. That's why they liked us.

Secrecy is the enemy of sanity and loving trust. If you keep secrets, you are an insane paranoic. Concealment is the seed source of every human conflict. Secrecy is always caused by guilt or fear. Liddy's parents were guilty about sex. And Nixon's parents. It drives them crazy when he secretly suspects that she's keeping secrets so he hires a private detective and—vice versus.

Let's break out of the huddle. Before J. Edgar Hoover there were no secret police in this country. Before World War II there was no C.I.A. and America was amazingly unconcerned with secrecy. The hidden sickness has become lethally epidemic in the last forty years.

Now comes the electronic revolution. Reveal-ation. Bugging equipment effective at long distances is inexpensive and easily available. Good. Liberals want stiff laws against bugging. It's the wrong move. Legalize everything. Legalize bugging. Let's forget artificial secrets and concentrate on the mysteries.

I can tell you bugging is nothing to worry about. I've been tapped, surveilled, tailed for ten years. In Algeria everyone knew of at least three taps on all international calls—Algerian, French and C.I.A. The Algerians knew every move we made. *That's why they liked us.* I was called in once by the Swiss Secret Service about some threats on my life. They offered me body guards. I looked at the chief agent and laughed. "Moi! Merci, non." The agent laughed with me. "Professor, the Swiss police never sleep. We watch over you twenty-four hours a day." Any real true intimate secrets are preserved in the tender codes of love. Privacy is woven with electric threads of contact that cannot be intercepted. Love has nothing to hide.

Secrecy is the original sin. Fig leaf in the Garden of Eden. The basic crime against love. The issue is fundamental. What a blessing that Iran-Scam has been uncovered to teach us the primary lesson. The purpose of life is to receive, process, and transmit energy. Communication fusion is the goal of life. Any star can tell you that. Communication is love. Secrecy, withholding the signal, hoarding, hiding, covering up the light is motivated by shame and fear, symptoms of the inability to love. Secrecy means that you think love is shameful and bad. Or that your nakedness is ugly. Or that you hide unloving, hostile feelings. Seed of paranoia and distrust.

Those who love have no need to hide their actions. As so often happens, the extreme wing is half right for the wrong reasons. They say primly: If you have done nothing wrong, you have no fear of being bugged. Exactly. But the logic goes both ways. Then F.B.I. files, and C.I.A. dossiers, and White House conversations should be open to all. Let every thing hang open. Let government

Let every thing hang open. Let government be totally visible. The last, the very last people to hide their actions should be the police and government.

be totally visible. The last, the very last people to hide their actions should be the police and government.

We operate on the assumption that everyone knows everything, anyway. There is nothing and no way to hide. This is the acid message. We're all on cosmic T.V. every moment. We all play starring roles in the galactic broadcast: This Is Your Life. I remember the early days of neurological uncovering, desperately wondering where I could go to escape. Run home, hide under the bed, in the closet, in the bathroom? No way. The relentless camera "I" follows me everywhere. We can only keep secrets from ourselves.

We laugh at government bugging. Let the poor, information-starved, bored, creatures listen to our converstions, tape our laughter, tap our transmissions. Maybe it will turn them on. Perhaps they'll get the message of the Cybernetic Age. "All information is free. All information is useful. There is nothing to fear from accurate communication."

The Curse of the Oval Room

August 1973
Folsom Prison

Power corrupts, rots, destroys, curses those who impose their rules upon others. We can only explain the addictive inability of politicians to recognize this historical fact as another one of those weird and faulty wirings that incapacitate the crippled nervous systems of our species.

Before 1914, the one throne of planetary power was contested by the kingdoms of Europe. After World War II the one crown passed to the Presidency of the United States. The word "crown" is not a metaphor but a scientific construct referring to a confirmable neurological state. Enormous psychic energies are directed towards the person who assumes the position of global power-holder. Unless this person possesses extraordinary psychological strength, clarity, and flexibility, his neurology blows a fuse. It is not altogether fanciful to refer to the "curse" of power that crazes all but those rare sovereigns who are genetically prepared for the responsibility. It is one of the many paradoxes of power that it can never be safely bought. The strength to rule is a neuro-genetic gift.

Since the time of Woodrow Wilson (Nixon's broken hero, by the way) twelve men have ruled the world from the Oval Room of the White House. Three have died in office—Harding, Roosevelt, and Kennedy. Six lived out their days crippled by scandal or failure—Wilson, Hoover, Johnson, Nixon, Carter and Reagan. The remaining three—Coolidge, Truman, and Eisenhower—also teach us something about the enigmatic, humbling pursuit of puissance.

Power corrupts, rots, destroys, curses those who impose their rules upon others.

And in the background the wailing Cassandra keen of Martha Mitchell: "John and I had everything going for us until he went to Washington. Now we've lost everything." It's a God-damned Greek morality play. Two days before the Nancy Reagan expose I wondered how many more disasters must come down before the writing in the sky becomes clear.

The Fall of Representative Government

September 1973
Folsom Prison

Americans, reeling with premonition, look around for a hero, an untainted leader. Let me tell you the good news. There won't be one. Politics is too important now to be turned over to ambitious politicians and adversary-process lawyers. The wise administration of social and economic affairs requires temperamental and intellectual characteristics notably absent in those who are driven to seek power. Do you really want to know what causes our political secrecy problems? Representative government. Elective democracy: one person is selected to "represent" others. Government by proxy. Even in the most liberal democracy, no one can represent someone else. (The non-representative nature of totalitarian governments is even more unwieldy.)

We have been robot-trained to believe that democracy as practiced in this country is something sacred. Everything we have been taught is dangerously wrong. Our history books are self-serving fabrications. Everything printed in our newspapers ia a selective fraud. (I know that you know this, but we have to keep reminding ourselves.)

Representative government as practiced today is a brief and now outmoded historical phase designed to bridge the period between the rise of industrial states and the emergence of globe-linking electrical-electronic communication.

The generic definition of democracy is equal voice for each citizen. In the town meeting or in the city-state participative democracy worked. As the industrial state emerged, the practice of selecting representatives to be sent to the distant capital became an inevitable step. An ominous division of labor developed. A class of secretive professional politicians.

The American Constitution was written in a late-stone-age, pre-mechanical, horse-power, slave-holding period. The articles which set up the mechanics of government are dangerously archaic.

The American Constitution was written in a late-stone-age, pre-mechanical, horse-power, slave-holding period. The preamble to the Constitution, which states the aim of the game, still stands as a good computer program. But the articles of the Constitution, which set up the mechanics of government, are dangerously archaic. Senators elected every six years to represent two million people? A president elected every four years to represent 140 million people? This slow, cumbersome system was necessary when it took two weeks for the news to travel from New Orleans to Boston. Representative government by strangers and political party partisanship is outdated. Most Americans have never met their representative—indeed do not know his name. Government by law is an unworkable bureaucratic cliche.

The political model should be based on the nervous system: 140 billion neurons each hooked to an electric network. Electronic communication makes possible direct participatory democracy. Every citizen has a voting card which he or she inserts in voting machine and central computers register and harmonize the messages from every component part. Neurological politics eliminates parties, politicians, campaigns, campaign expenditures. The citizen votes like a neuron fires when it has a signal to communicate. The voices of the citizenry continually inform civil service technicians who carry out the will, not of the majority (a vicious and suicidal elevation of the mediocracy) but of each citizen. Every citizen has personal computer appliances one-tenth as powerful as the government's.

The Return of Individual Sovereignty

September 1973
Folsom Prison

Technology can be used to reduce individual freedom and to enhance the power of politicians controlling centralized governments. B.F. Skinner, the conditioning psychologist, speaks for the authoritarian technocrats advocating a control "beyond human freedom and dignity." The control people realize that an industrial-assembly line society requires total cooperation and docile obedience of the citizenry. Skinner's system for conditioning children requires total control of reward-punishment and complete secrecy about the methods involved. The vulnerability of any technological system of totalitarian mind control is the prerequisite of secrecy and unanimity. One dissident electronic-media expert, one libertarian psychologist can jam the system. I did it here. Sakharov is doing it in Russia. Only by understanding the principles and techniques involved can one avoid being computerized and conditioned.

The challenge and glory of cybernetic democracy is this: society can no longer allow one person to feel abused, persecuted, ignored. Everyone must understand how the open neural network works and have access to it. Listen. Last August I was invited to dinner by an influential Swiss politician who said he could arrange for political asylum in his canton. He was a secret sexual dissident, his apartment a cozy culture cave, walls lined with classical albums, and upholstered with leather-bound, never-opened books. My host cooked and served a gourmet dinner. I sat at the head of the table drinking wine, listening to six businessmen explain why Switzerland should vote "yes" on the

The glory of electronic technological scientific culture is that it operates according to the laws of nature and cannot be permanently captured by the artificial laws of politics.

referendum to authorize the manufacture and sales of arms. "It's not the money, it's the market principle; if the underdeveloped countries want to buy arms why shouldn't we profit." Etc.

I had been shooting screen tests for the role of Harry Haller in the film production of Hesse's **Steppenwolf**.

Then the party fell to discussing the shoot-out at the Munich Olympics. Everyone clucked and shook their heads.

I was totally programmed by the Hesse-Haller script. You remember the bust-of-Goethe-scene? Haller tells the professor that he is a drunken, outlaw philosopher unfit for social appearances. Unhappily none of the dinner guests had read *Steppenwolf*. It's untidy when the other actors don't realize that we're playing out the classic script, almost word for word.

I recited the Haller-Hesse lines:

"Munich, my friends, is neither good nor bad. It's an inevitable, undeniable symptom. A meteorological signal. Too bad that ten men were slain, the games disrupted, and the very word **Olympics** now and forever associated with political despair. Will the lesson be learned? The same week a thousand peasants bombed to death in Vietnam, half a million Pakistani-Bangladesh rot in prison camps, while the affluent gather in Munich to play flag-waving contests for national prestige. The lesson of the Munich Olympics is that in this technological world as long as any one person hurts or even believes that he hurts we have to stop games-as-usual and pay attention to the wounded member. Life on this planet is one living organism and the pain of the smallest cluster of cells can cripple the whole. Hijackings, electronic sabotage, crime waves, biological-germ guerilla coups, are the initial symptoms."

I'm walking on the prison yard with Wayne, who asks me about the lesson of Watergate. I tell him that we are going to replace representative government by proxy and substitute electronic voting. Every citizen registers his or her signal. Wayne's a realist. He shakes his head. "Of course, it's the only solution, but it's too far out. It will scare people." I tell him that it's not so new. The stock market works exactly on that principle. Continual votes of confidence. Ongoing registry of opinion. Tell people they all own an equal share in the government. Wayne shakes his head. "Keep thinking." (People would be surprised at the level of prison conversations. All I ever hear are discussions about the great political and philosophic questions and their solutions.)

Okay, how about this? There is one thing that every American agrees on. The dishonesty and incompetence of politicians. Any politician who runs for office on the platform that he's going to do everything he can to take power

Language, thought and custom are becoming electrically energized. Those born into the electric culture will soon learn how to govern themselves according to the laws of information.

away from politicians and return it to the people is going to ride a powerful wave. The number one issue is the inability of the government to govern. A new constitutional convention charged with the responsibility of creating a governmental structure which utilizes electronic expression of individual opinion will get the country alive and laughing again.

The glory of electronic technology and scientific culture is that they operate according to the laws of nature and cannot be permanently captured by the artificial laws of politics. The medium is the evolutionary message. Science and computer technology cannot be controlled by a national leader or restrained by national boundaries. Language, thought and custom are becoming electrically energized. Those born into the electronic culture will soon learn how to govern themselves according to the laws of information.

Platitude tells us that Nixon will never recover from Watergate. Neither will the country. Competitive politics is dying. Ollie North is a crewcut dinosaur. The secret is out. Tap our wire any time you want, Liddy. We're broadcasting for you, too. We've got continuous power output, direct coupling, audible spectrum, low noise transmission, high circuit reliability, superb capture rate, excellent selectivity. If we had known you were hiding in the paleolithic bushes we would have invited you to tune in. It's the new Hi-Fi, Psi-Phy, polychromatic, multi-channel planetary network and we're all linked up love.

How To Wash Brains

December 1975
San Diego Federal Prison

The fight for Patty Hearst's mind is symptomatic of the world-wide battle for the control of consciousness.

★

"Mon, Dad—I'm OK. I had a few scrapes and stuff, but they washed them up, and they're getting OK... I heard that Mom is really upset and that everybody was at home, and I hope this puts you a little bit at ease... I want to get out of here, but the only way I'm going to do it is if we do it their way... I just want to get out of here and see everyone again and be back with Steve."

February 12, 1974. The speaker is Patty Hearst. Although she has been held prisoner by the Symbionese Liberation Army guerillas for eight days, she sounds relatively normal, and the tape is reassuring to her parents.

A second tape is released by the S.L.A. 49 days later, and everything changes. A new voice, that of a stranger named Tania, is speaking and the words are hostile:

"I know for sure yours and Mom's interests are never the interests of the people. You, a corporate liar, of course, will say that you don't know what I'm talking about, but I ask you then to prove it. Tell the poor and oppressed people of this nation what the corporate state is about to do. Warn black and poor people that they are about to be murdered down to the last man, woman and child."

This tape is accompanied by the famous photo of Tania holding a tommy gun, standing before the Symbionese seven-headed cobra.

Escape from our robothood happens when we learn to take control of our nervous systems and to reprogram our individual realities.

Randolph Hearst, Father of the Year and top manager of a mass-media propaganda machine that has helped domesticate millions of minds during the past century, comes before the TV cameras and says, unconvincingly, "We had her 20 years; they've only had her 60 days. I don't believe she's going to change her philosophy that quickly and that permanently."

Two weeks later, Tania is photographed robbing a bank with her new comrades, and the third tape, even more vehement, describes the parents she had wanted to see again as "pigs" and Steve Weed, the lover she had wanted to return to, as "a clown" and a "sexist pig."

Tania would live to change her mind again, but obviously she would never again be the original Patty Hearst.

During the trial of Lieutenant William Calley, it was obvious to millions all over the world that the U.S. Army was seeking to disguise its own guilt by making a scapegoat out of a singularly naive young man. It was not obvious to Calley, however. "I'm for the Army all the way," he told reporters. "I'm behind it, a member of it. The Army comes first. No matter how much I could help my own defense, I won't make any derogatory statement about the Army."

Rusty Calley was, before induction, an unattached, marginally employed drifter—a bellhop, a dishwasher, a pieceworker—until he underwent the brain-changing ordeal of infantry basic training. Today he dutifully defends his brainwashers as robotically as Tania once defended hers, and he justifies mass murder in the jargon of the true believer.

Between the time of her arrest for pointing a gun at Gerald Ford last summer and her conviction last November, Lynette "Squeaky" Fromme did nothing to aid her own defense and everything to broadcast the philosophy of Charlie Manson, in whose commune she had been brainwashed. Nothing said by the judge or by her own lawyer could make Fromme's legal situation real or important to her. All that she cared about was having the attention of the media in order to broadcast Manson's message.

There is nothing to indicate any special weakness in Patty or Rusty or Squeaky. They were quite normal young Americans until they came into the ambience of, respectively, the S.L.A., the U.S. Army and the Manson family. This is the first lesson we must understand.

Brainwashing, like malaria, is a disease of exposure. Put people in a malarial environment and most of them will get malaria. Put them in a brainwashing institution and most of them will get brainwashed.

The four survival brains are progressively bleached out and reimprinted in the relatively simple mechanical process called brainwashing.

The concept of "washing" is, of course, unscientific and crude. The brain is not a dirty garment but a bio-electric computer—a living network of over 110 billion nerve cells capable of $10^{2783000}$ interconnections, a number higher than the total of all the atoms in the universe. In this elegant, microminiaturized computer, more than 100,000,000 processes are programmed every minute.

The brain and the nervous system, like the rest of the body, are designed and programmed by the genetic code. The human being, like all other life forms, is primarily "a giant robot created by DNA to make more DNA," as Nobel geneticist Herman J. Muller has observed.

We are all neurogenetic robots. And, however unpleasant it may be for Christian theologians or sentimental humanists to acknowledge this, there is no escape from our robothood unless and until we first recognize the fact. Only then can we learn to take control of our nervous systems to reprogram our individual programs.

A basic example of brain programming, which helps us to understand Rusty, Squeaky, Patty and ourselves, concerns the newborn giraffe whose mother was shot by hunters. The baby giraffe—in accordance with its genetic program—imprinted the first large moving object it saw, which happened to be the hunters' jeep. It followed, vocalized to, tried to suckle and eventually to mate with the unresponsive vehicle. The giraffe's survival instincts were hooked to that jeep.

The human being also imprints—or hooks its neural equipment to—external objects. Among humans, these imprints come in four stages:

1. The infant biosurvival circuit, concerned with safety-danger signals here and now.
2. The older-infant (toddler) circuit, or *ego*; concerned with motion and emotion;
3. The student, verbal-symbolic circuit, or *mind*; concerned with language and knowledge;
4. The adult sociosexual circuit, or *personality*; concerned with domestic behavior.

These four circuits are the four brains that are progressively bleached out and reimprinted in the relatively simple mechanical process called brainwashing. The process is simple, because the original imprinting of these circuits was also relatively simple.

The first circuit, or **biosurvival brain,** is activated at birth. Its function is to seek

Throughout human life, when the biosurvival brain flashes danger, all other mental activities cease. To create a new imprint, first reduce the subject to the state of infancy, i.e., first-brain vulnerability.

food, air, warmth, comfort and to retreat from what is toxic, harsh, or dangerous. The biosurvival circuit of the animal nervous system is DNA-programmed to seek a comfort-safety zone around a mothering organism. If a mother is not present, the closest substitute in the environment will be chosen.

For the newborn giraffe, a four-wheel jeep was fixated. In one of Konrad Lorenz's ethological studies, a gosling that could not find the rounded white body of a goose to fixate imprinted a round, white ping-pong ball.

Throughout human life; when the biosurvival brain flashes danger, all other mental activities cease. This is of key importance in brain programming: to create a new imprint, first reduce the subject to the state of infancy, i.e., first-brain vulnerability.

The initial step in this process is isolation of the victim. A small, dark room is ideal, since the social, emotional and mental techniques that formerly ensured survival will not work there. The longer the person is isolated in such a state, the more vulnerable to new imprint he or she becomes. As Dr. John C. Lilly has pointed out, it takes only a few minutes of true isolation before anxiety appears and only a few hours before hallucinations begin, and the victim is ready to be imprinted with a new protective, maternal object.

It is no paradox that even the captor who is imposing this brainwashing on the unwilling subject can be the one imprinted. The victim is forced by instincts—biochemical programs—many millions of years old to seek this imprint and to hook it to whatever external entity comes closest to the mother archetype. For a human prisoner, any two-legged being who brings food will serve. This is called the Stockholm Syndrome.

The second circuit, the **emotional brain**, or ego, is initially imprinted when the child begins to use muscle power to crawl, walk, master gravity, overcome physical obstacles and manipulate others politically. The muscles that perform these functions are very quickly imprinted with what become chronic, lifelong reflexes. Depending on the accidents of environment, this imprint will make for either a strong, dominating ego or a weak, fearful, dependent or hostile ego.

Status in the pack or the tribe is assigned on the basis of an unconsciouss signaling system in which these muscle reflexes are crucial. The emotional games or cons, listed in the popular game-manuals of Dr. Eric Berne and the transactional analysts, are second-brain imprints, or standard mammalian politics.

To re-create second-brain imprint vulnerability in an adult, the subject must be made to feel like a clumsy infant. The subject's neurological scoreboard must clearly register the message, "I am one foot tall, ignorant, inept, frightened and wrong. *They* are six feet tall, wise, clever, powerful and right."

Helplessness can be escalated to panic by means of terror tactics. In Costa-

Basic imprint vulnerability occurs when the subject comes to believe, "I have no choice; they can do anything they want with me."

Gavras' film *The Confession*, the Communist brainwashers take the subject from his cell, put a noose around his neck and lead him to a place where he expects to be hanged; some African tribes take candidates for "initiation" and bury them alive for hours.

Basic imprint vulnerability occurs when the subject comes to believe, "I have no choice; they can do anything they want with me." At this point, the emotional brain hooks into the victim internalizes a rank in the pecking order under the protection of the most powerful figure available.

The third brain, or **rational mind**, is imprinted when the child begins to use artifacts and to ask questions. The imprint sites are the nine laryngeal muscles that are used in speech and a neural feed-back loop between the right hand and the left cortex, which is used in examining, classifying and rearranging the objects of the environment. The entire edifice of science, art and knowledge is built on this foundation.

The quickest way to reimprint the third brain is to detach the victim from those who share the same language, symbols and doctrines by placing the victim in a situation where his usual verbal skills and physical dexterity won't work, where he has to imprint new signals and skills in order to survive. For example, it is well known that the best way to learn a foreign language is by living with those who speak that language only: Hook the first-circuit survival needs (food, shelter) and the second-circuit status needs (security, recognition) to the third-circuit necessity of mastering the new tongue.

Conversely, the proverbial Englishman who dressed for dinner every night in his lonely tropical hut was no fool. He was keeping an English bubble around him by constantly reaffirming an English reality, and so avoiding being engulfed in the reality of the natives. It is not unusual for a man to become a Communist when he lives with Communists, or a convict when he lives with convicts. In fact, it requires delicate neurological engineering to remain oneself under such conditions.

The fourth brain, or **personality**, is activated and imprinted at adolescence, when the DNA signal awakens the sexual apparatus. The teenager becomes the bewildered possessor of a new body and a new neural circuit hooked to orgasm and sperm-egg fusion. The pubescent human, like any other mammal, lurches about in a state of mating frenzy, every neuron gasping for the sex object.

Imprint vulnerability is acute, and the first sexual cues to turn on the adolescent nervous system remain fixed for life and forever define the individual's sexual reality. We should not be surprised, therefore, at the various

> **Everywhere, in every society, the sexual brain is ruthlessly domesti-
> cated, channeled into tribal productivity. Socially approved orgasm is
> directed toward monogamous procreation; pleasure directed orgasm
> is denounced.**

fetishes that are so easily acquired at these sensitive moments. In fact, we can
tell precisely at what period in time a person was imprinted by noting which
fetishes continue to turn him on: black garters, booze, cool jazz and crewcuts
define one whole generational imprint group, just as sleeping bags, Mick Jagger,
grass and tight jeans define another.

When Sinatra sings at Las Vegas, the menopausal fan ignores his wrinkles
and double chin and the neurons kick over in reflex rapture. The younger
generation is amused and bored: "What's that balding old man got to do with
sex?" No group ever understands the fetishes of another sexual-imprint group.

It is important for the brainwasher to understand that sexual behavior is
intensely influenced by social-domestic morals. The tribe *always* surrounds
sperm-egg exchange with fierce threats and violent taboos—to the degree that
most people don't even know that the word **morals** refers to anything other
than sexual no-nos.

Everywhere, in every society, the sexual brain is ruthlessly domesticated,
channeled into tribal productivity. Socially approved orgasm is directed toward
monogamous procreation; pleasure directed orgasm is denounced and the
practitioners are often persecuted.

Rewiring the sexual circuits, then, breaks the domestic bond, fissions the
domesticated personality and allows for the creation of a new bond to a
different subculture and to its heretical sexual value system. Such reimprinting
of the erotic brain can be a most effective mind-washing technique but only as
an adjunct to the basic reprogramming of the first- and second-brain circuits of
security and ego status. For example, if Cinque had raped Patty Hearst the first
night of her captivity, a strong revulsion on her part would probably have
occurred. However, *after* the subject has come to look to the brainwasher for
biosecurity, physical support, emotional reality definition, then a sexual
seduction can imprint a new erotic field.

In order to maintain one's reality bubble, it is necessary to surround oneself
with tribal reassurance. Most human communication is embarrassingly
primitive, consisting of endless variations on "I'm still here. Are you still there?"
(hive solidarity and "Nothing has really changed" (hive business as usual).
Isolation, the first step in brainwashing, removes this protective bubble. When
the subject no longer receives feedback—"We're all still here; nothing has
changed"—the imprints begin to fade.

Explorers and shipwrecked sailors who have survived prolonged isolation,
Dr. Lilly has noted, are quite shy after being rescued. They are literally afraid of
human conversation—sometimes for weeks—because they know that what they

Once the subject looks to the re-programmer for biosecurity and ego support, just as the infant looks to its parents, any third-brain ideology can be impressed on the vulnerable neurons.

will say might sound insane to the domesticated ordinary adult; their imprints have faded and they are in the unconditioned free-floating world of the yogi or the mystic. It takes many days, at least, to reimprint their social bubble.

Similar imprint vulnerability and return to infancy occurs in many cases of prolonged hospitalization, an ominous fact that many medical technicians do not understand. Some patients are literally brainwashed into becoming lifelong invalids—a classic case of second-brain helplessness—and are accused by the staff of being malingerers, a label that shifts the blame from the incompetent technicians to the helpless victim.

It is the function of our mind-programs to focus, to select, to narrow down, to choose, from an infinity of possibilities, the biochemical imprints which determine the tactics and strategies that ensure survival in *one* place, status in *one* tribe. The infant is genetically prepared to learn *any* language, master *any* skill, play *any* sex role; in a very short time, however, he becomes rigidly fixated to accept, follow and mimic the limited offerings of his social and cultural environment.

In this process, each of us pays a heavy price. Survival and status means forfeiting the infinite possibilities of unconditioned consciousness. The domesticated personality inside the social bubble is a trivial fragment of the potentials for experience and intelligence innate in the 110-billion-cell human biocomputer. We have literally been robbed blind; we have literally taken leave of our senses; we are literally only slightly more conscious than any other herd animal.

The brainwasher's job is simple, then, because it consists only of substituting one set of robotic circuits for another set. Once the subject looks to the re-programmer for biosecurity and ego support, just as the infant looks to its parents, any third-brain ideology can be impressed on the vulnerable neurons.

Because we are all imprinted by our own social bubbles, it isn't generally recognized that each reality map held by humans—however eccentric and paranoid—makes nearly as much sense as any other. People are vegetarians or nudists or Communists or snake worshipers for the same reasons that other people are Catholics or Republicans or liberals or Nazis.

During imprint vulnerability, anybody can be switched from one system to another. We can easily be induced to go from intoning "Hare Krishna" to "Jesus died for our sins" to "Kill the pigs," and to find meaning in each of the implied ideologies. The next step is for the brainwashers to persuade us that anybody who doesn't see the world according to a particular reality map is wicked, or stupid, or insane.

After programming a third-brain bubble around the subject, a complete brainwashing procedure must then reimprint sexual drives and taboo systems. It

The ironic truth is that our concept of reality is so fragile that it collapses in a matter of days if we do not have continual spot announcements reminding us of who we are and that our reality is still there.

is here that governmental brainwashers are amusingly inept, as compared with outlaw bands. Governments are prudish, uptight and sexually cold, because domestication depends on directing genital passions away from individual gratification and into the nuclear family—or, in modern insectoid socialisms, away from the individual *and* the family, and into collective hive productivity.

Sexual reprogramming can imprint either a new sex role (as when the Mau Mau insisted that would-be members perform an act of homosexuality, in order to sever themselves from family-oriented sex) or a sex-avoidance role (as with nuns, who become brides of Christ and convert sexual charges into religious tingles). The military and the prison systems, after isolating people from ordinary social reality, allow and tacitly approve asocial sexual imprints, whether heterosexual or homosexual; a year's worth of sperm on cell or barracks sheets is a year's programming in anti-domesticity. Similarly, everybody knows that the classic attraction of military life has been the opportunity for socially approved sexual license, including whorehouse adventures and the rape of enemy women—an enticing program to a young male primate.

(The great mystery that puzzled and irritated the menopausal males who ruled America in the Sixties—why weren't young males eager for the adventure of Vietnam?—is easily answered in a neurological context: The new sexual imprints of the marijuana revolution made it unnecessary and unaesthetic to go to Saigon to get righteously laid.)

Continual follow-up is necessary to reinforce any new reality imprint. The ironic truth is that our concept of reality is so fragile that it collapses in a matter of days if we do not have continual spot announcements reminding us of who we are and that our reality is still there.

The military accordingly constructs a military-reality island for its personnel. Every successful brainwasher, whether Synanon, a Jesus cult, a Hindu swami movement, a Manson-type family, or a militant terrorist group, creates a similar reality island; once a person joins, he is in all the way, 24 hours a day, seven days a week. Similarly, revolutionary governments dare not relax censorship or permit free communications in their drive to wash out the old imprints and reinforce new ones. Foreign or dissenting signals cannot, therefore, be tolerated.

This reality-island context helps us to appreciate the ease with which the Army brainwashed Calley.

A confused, ineffective youth joins the Army; during basic training, he is isolated from civilian society and all reinforcers of domesticated-herd imprints; his food, clothing and shelter are provided by the Army; and new authority

The hippie movement, with its estimated 35,000,000 pot smokers, can be viewed as an experiment in self-induced brain change. Neurotransmitter drugs perform the same function as isolation, as they weaken or suspend the users' old imprints.

figures make him feel helpless and inferior. Once Rusty has been reduced to an infant state and made totally dependent on the new father figures, he is allowed to work his way up in the new pecking order and to become one of the elect. After a few weeks of being made to feel one foot tall, helpless and clumsy, he is given weekend leave to explore the new soldier morality of easy camaraderie and socially approved casual sex. (And where else in straight America is casual sex so enthusiastically approved?) Day after day, Rusty's third brain is being programmed with military jargon, military concepts, military reality. When he encounters civilians on the street during weekend leaves, they seem alien.

Rusty has now been fully incorporated into the Army reality bubble. When his superior officer, Medina, shouts "Kill!" Calley will not ask about the Articles of War, the Nuremberg precedents, the ethics of Sunday school—they belong to other reality islands. He kills. The whole function of the reimprinting in basic training has been to ensure that Calley will obey in such situations.

The robotization of Squeaky Fromme by Charles Manson was just as simple, although the source of Manson's powers has been misunderstood.

It is insufficient, first of all, to say that Manson—and his powers over the family members—was a product of the drug culture. The hippie movement, with its estimated 35,000,000 pot smokers, can, in fact, be viewed as an enormous, mostly amateurish experiment in *self-induced* brain change. Neurotransmitter drugs perform the same function as isolation, as they weaken or suspend the users' old imprints.

This is exactly why conservatives dread dope: They do not want the younger half of the population experimenting with consciousness alteration, ego change, mind metamorphoses and sex-role roulette. If the military had pioneered the use of grass as an adjunct to imprinting military obedience, social attitudes would probably have been reversed. Conservatives would have defended Cannabis with the same pragmatism that they brought to the dropping of napalm bombs, and radical dissidents would have dreaded Cannabis as much as they fear wire tapping.

Manson used drugs as but one brainwashing tool, and he did so for ends alien to the drug culture. While other gurus of the sixties used drugs to rewire their followers for the peace-love-ecology trip, Manson used the same drugs to imprint his family for fascism, racism, sexism. Manson could have become a platoon sergeant in the Green Berets.

In **Helter Skelter**, prosecutor Bugliosi lists the programs Sergeant Manson employed with his drugs: first-brain fear and isolation from straight society; second-brain communal status and rote-repetition of emotional phrases from

The reality bubble Manson later created at the Spahn Movie Ranch near Los Angeles was the stereophonic 3-D dream of every pimp-doper-convict.

from the ever-convenient Bible; third-brain occult teachings; fourth-brain guilt-free sex. In **The Family**, Ed Sanders adds that female members were usually initiated with an LSD trip, during which Charlie performed oral sex on them several times.

Of course, Manson's hypnotic power also derived from the pathetic fact that he was the most brainwashed robot of them all; Manson not only followed but believed in the blood-drenched script of the book of *Revelations*—the great beast, the war between good and evil, the last judgment. Instant apocalypse defined Manson's third-brain reality bubble; prison taught him how to enforce it.

Manson spent 17 of his first 32 years in prison; isolation behind walls and bars reinfantizied his survival brain; competing gangs of cons and guards impressed the most violent mammalian politics on his emotional brain; a weird variety of fundamentalist and racist ideologies was fed to his symbolic brain; and anything *except* domesticated reproductive sex programmed his erotic brain. The reality bubble Manson later created at the Spahn Movie Ranch near Los Angeles was the stereophonic 3-D dream of every pimp-doper-convict.

The S.L.A. hideout of general field marshal Cinque, another graduate of the California archipelago, was the Marxist version of the same convict fantasy: guns stolen cars, girls, obedience, senseless killings. S.L.A. kidnappers merely applied to Patty Hearst the standard brainwashing techniques learned by Cinque in the brain-change prisons of California: first, the physical shock of kidnap, the disorientation of the car-trunk ride and confinement in a small, dark room. Then came Cinque's visits to the isolation cell, and the transformation in his role from that of captor into that of the source of Patty's biological survival. The motherlike Cinque brought food and drink; the fatherlike Cinque told her sternly that her survival depended on his whims. Patty is reduced to the status of a suckling infant, one foot tall in a six-foot-tall world.

Throughout life, when the first brain flashes danger, all other mental activities cease.

Once Patty had imprinted Cinque in place of her distant parents and unavailable lover, he introduced the new symbol system, the new reality bubble. His powerful laryngeal muscles filled the air of the tiny room with sonorous, poetic rhetoric of the ghetto, the prison and the underworld, strengthened by Marxist apocalyptical theology. The same mindwashing has been experienced by thousands of runaways and dropouts who, during the past decade, found themselves in the crowded, womb-warren pads of Haight-Ashbury or the East Village, vulnerable to a new, hip version of the ancient anarchist, outlaw symbolism.

(The importance of *funk* cannot be overestimated in these cases. The brain of

The importance of funk cannot be overestimated in these cases. The brain of the baby—and of the reinfantized adult—craves warmth, texture, skin smell, sloppy-moist contact.

the baby—and of the reinfantized adult—craves warmth, texture, skin smell, sloppy-moist contact. The newborn correctly equates dirt and smell with survival, and so does the hairy, aromatic hippie who thrives on incense, candlelight, sleeping bags, crash pads. Domesticated moralists who denounce this rank way of life do not realize that, to the reinfantized brain, funk means survival bliss.)

The culmination of Patty Hearst's reprogramming was the new sexual reality imposed on her fourth brain. In a curiously naive account of Patty's captivity, an anonymous S.L.A. member has unwittingly outlined the brainwashing procedure:

"There are many people who still cannot comprehend Tania's swift evolution from sheltered bourgeois to freedom fighter. We wish to end all metaphysical speculation around brainwashing and sexual enslavement."

With this disclaimer, the S.L.A. account found in the Harris' San Francisco hideout proceeds to describe classic brainwashing techniques. "In the beginning, we provided for Tania's basic needs: shelter, food, clothing, medical attention and news from the outside. Although we considered sex a basic human need, our commitment to not exploit her sexually, coupled with her over-all status as a P.O.W., denied Tania the freedom to have sex with another person. But later on . . . as she became more integrated into the day-to-day aspects of cell life, we tried to treat Tania as an equal. It was only natural that with increased personal interaction . . . these relations would develop sexually."

Tania's S.L.A. imprints, reinforced by 24-hours-a-day immersion in the new tribe's reality, seem to have remained durable until the Los Angeles shoot-out. Jack Scott's description of Tania in the subsequent months of cross-country flight, however, reveals a restless, irritable, unsettled person. The chief programmer, Cinque, was gone and Patty/Tania eventually returned, with the instincts of a migratory bird, to San Francisco, the locale of her two birthplaces.

After arrest, a campaign to reprogram Patty yet again was initiated by her captors. Again her biosurvival needs were satisfied by her jailers; her ego status depended on pleasing them, and ceaseless effort was made to induce her to verbalize anew the symbol system of her parents. Tania's liberated sexual imprints, predictably enough, led her to marry her security guard!

The hope for Patty Hearst—as for the rest of us brainwash victims—is to realize how robot-imprinting works, to laugh at the embarrassing insight and to start choosing our own imprints.

Was Rusty Calley, the Florida drifter, guilty of murder? No. The crimes were

Brainwashing is happening to all of us all of the time. Knowledge of brain function is our only protection against it. The solutions to our predicament are neurological. We must assume responsibility for our nervous systems.

committed by Lieutenant Calley, a brainwashed robot programmed by the Army to kill on command.

Was Lynette Alice Fromme guilty of attempted assassination? No. The Sacramento gun was carried by Squeaky Fromme, a brainwashed robot from Charles Manson's zombie platoon.

Was Patty Hearst guilty of any crime? No. Tania is a brain-changed product of the neurotechnology of Drill Instructor Cinque.

But let us pursue the neurology of guilt a few steps farther. Who taught Charles Manson and Cinque the techniques of brain change, as well as their philosophies of violence? The prison system did. And who supports the prisons that robotized Manson and Cinque, along with the Army that mechanized Calley? Taxpaying citizens.

Our purpose here is not to provoke another round of liberal we're-all-guilty hand-wringing. Guilt, innocence, morality and will power have nothing to do with the neurological situation, which, in brief, is that we are all automatons responding automatically to imprinted realities of an embarrassingly arbitrary nature. The motivations of criminality and law-abiding virtue, of violence and love, of domestication and deviance, of laziness and industry, promiscuity and prudery, stupidity and cleverness, are always random neurological imprints. What impresses the neurons during imprint vulnerability is what gets imprinted.

Guilt, innocence, punishment, forgiveness, law and order, rehabilitation—all constitute the mythology that masks the simple reality of badly wired robots bumping into one another. Most agonizing and supposedly intractable social problems are caused solely by our ignorance of the brain's capacity for rote repetition and abrupt change.

Brainwashing is happening to all of us all of the time. Knowledge of brain function is our only protection against it. The solutions to our predicament are neurological. We must assume responsibility for our nervous systems. Our robothood can remain static if we endlessly repeat the imprints of infancy to adolescence, or it can be drastically altered by brainwashers without our consent, or we can take control of our nervous systems. If we *don't* assume this personal responsibility, somebody else will; if we *do* take over the control board, we can each be any person we want to be.

The Neuropolitics of Courage:
A Brief Encounter with Charles Manson

Commodore Dylan, Agent from Central Intelligence assigned to earth, third planet of a G-type Star, sits on the bench of the holding cell of Soledad Prison, dressed in the white jump suit worn by transferees. On his left, John O'Neill, a slick good-looking big-city Irishman down for ten to life for murder two. To his right, a tall, slim, pretty cowboy named Ted with Indian cheekbones, and a deep tan. Ted babbles evasively. He has been in and out of the joint for years and has the reputation of being a professional fuck-up. ("He ain't playing with a full deck," whispers O'Neill. "He's one of the girls and a snitch, too.") The three hold one-way tickets to the Dark Tower, and that has formed a bond among them. The Dark Tower is Folsom, a trans-Einsteinian Black Hole in the Earth Galaxy from which nothing ever escapes but feeble red radiation.

Dylan had done some primatology research in Hollywood after the Tate-La Bianca murders and was fascinated by the wave of fright that swept through the film colony. The chic reaction was to install gate locks, which were opened by remote control after visitors identified themselves over an intercom. Whatever solace this arrangement provided, it certainly would not have thwarted the creepy-crawly Mansonites, who avoided the gate at the Tate house because they suspected that it was electrified. So Dylan wrote a memoir for *OUI* magazine to show that none of the human fears that Manson systematically exploited can be neutralized by external defenses. These terrors, he wrote, are internal neurological reactions and, in order to understand Manson, one must understand the neurology of human fear.

Before we can understand Manson, we must realize that a prison system is a microcosm of a culture and that the American prison system is run on raw fear and violence.

Manson, it was said, stimulated fear in others in order to gain power.

"One aspect of Manson's philosophy especially puzzled me: his strange attitude toward fear," Vincent Bugliosi says in *Helter Skelter*. "He not only preached that fear was beautiful, he often told the family that they should live in a constant state of fear. What did he mean by that? I asked Paul Watkins, (Manson's second-in-command).

"To Charlie, fear was the same thing as awareness," Watkins said. "The more fear you have, the more awareness, hence the more love. When you're really afraid, you come to 'Now.' And when you are at *Now*, you are totally conscious."

Let us give credit where credit is due: Manson's manipulation of fear has its roots in the paranoia behind the Cold War military posture, the antidrug scare campaigns, the addictive success of the most popular movies and crime shows, the actions of all bureaucracy and law-enforcement agencies, and the operation of our penal institutions.

Before we can understand Manson, we must realize that a prison system is a microcosm of a culture and that the American prison system is run on raw fear and violence.

The bus comes snorting into the Soledad parking area. The Folsom-bound trio is motioned outside to stand in the sun glare, waiting for the chains. Commodore Dylan recognizes the transport guards from previous trips: the burly black who likes to clean his automatic, the pink-faced John Wayne type, the sleek, mean sergeant.

"It's a hot day and a short ride and only a few of 'em. So we won't cuff 'em," says the sergeant.

"The Professor's an escape risk," says glum pink-face, rocking back and forth on his feet.

"Ah, he won't try a rabbit on us," purrs the sarge.

"Not until we make one mistake. Right?" says the black, looking at the Commodore coldly.

There are four other cons on the bus. All claim to have done time with the Commodore at joints he's never attended. "It's like Kennedy's PT-boat crew," he thinks.

The bus wheezes through Soledad's inner inspection gates and stops at the prison's main entrance. The guards dismount and wait while their guns are lowered in a basket from the tower. The bus chugs through the main entrance gate and Soledad is left behind.

The ride through California's central valley is a pleasant exploration. Blake

Once, when his unwitting snub of a gang member thrust him into the center of a confrontation, several hundred men armed with prison knives stood uneasily on the yard while negotiations were conducted. Naked adrenaline diplomacy.

said that the fool sees not the same tree that the wise man sees. The free see not the same tree that the convict sees.

The power and politics of fear are, unfortunately, beyond the experience of middleclass electroids, who let televised actors get their kicks for them. Only the cop, the prisoner and the ghetto veteran know the primal exhilaration of total alertness—which they must maintain in order to survive.

Dylan's education in this raw reality of fear came quickly on the main line of a pre-Folsom Gulag. Every morning he would leave his cell at 8:30, walk to the end of the cell block, wait to be unlocked and then lope down the half mile of main corridor to his work assignment. On this daily commute, he passed more than 50 inmates and guards. And each intersection demanded a conscious and precisely accurate social signal. Failure to say "Hey man" to this one, failure to smile at another, failure to stop for a quick "What's happening, man?" with the next, could set off a complex reaction that might mean death. On the other hand, he dared not look at this one, nor smile at that one, nor stop to talk to the next, lest another cycle of paranoia be set off.

Once, when his unwitting snub of a gang member thrust him into the center of a confrontation between opposing factions, several hundred men armed with prison knives stood uneasily on the yard while negotiations were conducted. That's reality politics. Naked adrenalin diplomacy.

At other times during his penal career, he was lucky enough to sit in prison yards and listen to scores of armed robbers describe their capers. Almost every one of these bandits admitted that the kick of the robbery came not from the money but from the panic aroused in the victim. "Man, those donkeys really piss their pants when you shove that big .45 in their faces." Loud laughter.

He also learned that the fear-generating bully who despises his victim also longs to submit to someone else. The most authoritarian person is comfortable only when supported by a stronger force. Manson, at the height of his Spahn Ranch power, was lost and confused without someone telling him what to do. As Manson told Bugliosi in a post-trial interview, "Prison has always been my home; I didn't want to leave it the last time, and you're only sending me back there."

The bus groans up to the Folsom perimeter. A grey-faced trusty with crablike motions runs to swing open the first gate. "All hope abandon, ye who enter here." The bus crosses the yard and parks by the entrance to the Folsom cell block.

The transit prisoners look out at the baseball diamond surrounded by concrete walks. The area is deserted except for a husky black man in a blue shirt who is watering the outfield, his rubber boots squishing in grassy puddles.

Intelligence [defined as the accurate, flexible reception, processing and transmission of signals] has no place in a fear society; the most dangerous and the strongest are automatically the smartest.

"Is this the main yard?" asks the Commodore. "It's not very large."

"Wait till you see it crowded with 2000 blue shirts," says a black slumped down in the front seat.

The escort guards jump down and confer over papers with prison guards. Everyone is bored.

"What happens now?"

"We gonna get put in the bottom tier," says the black. "We stay there till they decide we safe here. Like we don't have no enemies, you know. Except if they take any of us to 4A."

"What's 4A?" asks the Commodore.

"That's just the baddest place you can get," the black says, laughing. "The adjustment center, you know. That's where they stow the real badasses, too mean and violent for the main line. Or snitches who like ain't worth five minutes on the main line. Folsom is the bottom of the prison system, and 4A is the bottom of *that*. Here the 4A bulls now. That means one of us be heading for the hole."

Prison is the classic laboratory-training school for fear and fearlessness. The middle class is terrified of its raw jungle reality; it took four years of incarceration for Dylan to be able to understand that if you show fear, you are marked for continual physical coercion.

Since Charles Manson spent most of his adult life in prison, he was obviously well-educated in the fear tactics of physical threat ("I am dangerous"), emotional dominance ("I am strong") and symbol manipulation ("I am smarter than you").

Intelligence [defined as the accurate, flexible reception, processing and transmission of signals] has no place in a fear society; the most dangerous and the strongest are automatically the smartest. Subtlety, insight, sensitivity, complexity, tolerant exchange of facts are *verboten* in a totalitarian system. The prison gang leader never admits ignorance or allows himself to receive facts. Communication is governed by pecking order. No one listens. No one thinks.

The seven men in the bus look at one another appraisingly: Who will Iron Jaws drag down to the hole? The metal door of a newer concrete building opens and three guards walk down the steps toward the bus. Big muscular men, carrying clubs held to their wrists with leather thongs. One of the transit guards leans inside the door of the bus.

"Hey, Doc. Come out here."

"They got yo ass now," says the black. "Keep cool and you can talk your way out in a few weeks. Or years."

The Alchemist is led into a bare room with a counter running along the left side. There are eight large guards, each carrying a club. Their faces are blank. "Strip."

The Wizard nods to the commiserating faces of his fellow voyagers and descends from the bus. The afternoon sun steams off the concrete. There is a deserted, dead feeling.

The three club carriers look at him impersonally. One of them jerks his thumb in the direction of 4A.

The Philosopher, feeling suddenly quite thin and vulnerable, walks Biblically toward the metal door. He is flanked by two guards with clubs. A third covers his rear. At the entrance, a guard talks into a squawk box and the door clocks open noisily. They march into a long hallway running to the left.

One of the guards blows a whistle and two approaching convicts freeze.

The procession walks 20 feet down the hall and stops in front of another metal door. A guard bangs with his club against the steel. From within, another guard peers out through a peep-hole and the door opens. They are now inside a windowless room. Another door. The guard bangs again. Another face peers through another peephole. Now this door opens.

The Alchemist is led into a bare room with a counter running along the left side. There are eight large guards, each carrying a club. Their faces are blank. "Strip."

When Manson was released from prison in March 1967, he brought to the loose, open, gullible, happy, flower-child culture of the Haight-Ashbury the three fear-provoking skills he had learned in crime school: physical threat, emotional dominance and dogmatic repetition of symbols. To these primitive methods, however, he added the fourth and most effective source of his power: moral coercion.

Before the Sixties, most domesticated humans were unaware of the way in which moral threat determined their behavior. They were oblivious to the coerciveness of family, clan, church, school and civil law, and of how each tried to limit behavior to that which would benefit the hive, the clan, the species. In the Sixties, however, a cultural revolution occurred which allayed the fear that is variously known as sin, guilt, evil and taboo. Millions of young people—and some flexible older people—were left floating in an ethical vacuum. Into this void moved the spiritual promoters and ethical mafias—the soul fuckers.

America, in the past decade, became a spiritual Wild West, with San Francisco as its Dodge City; religious gang leaders and ethical gunslingers competed for control, among them the Diggers, black militants, hippie gurus, Hindu swamis, hedonic prophets, Jesus freaks, makeshift messiahs, health-food fanatics, soul pimps and hope dealers.

Millions of young people—and some flexible older people—were left floating in an ethical vacuum. Into this void moved the spiritual promoters and ethical mafias—the soul fuckers.

Into this Byzantine situation came Manson, fresh from the academy of fear, brandishing a book that cites the highest ethical authority to justify ritual murder, a 3000-year-old text loaded with prescription and pronunciamento designed to strike fear into nonbelievers: the book of *Revelation*.

Dylan, as ordered, removes the white jump suit, socks and the white track shoes purchased in Lucerne.

He stands naked and a guard approaches with a metal detector the size and shape of a ping-pong paddle, which is passed around his head, face, neck and body. The guard then moves the detector over the discarded clothes. Another tosses Dylan a tattered gray jump suit and cloth slippers, and points to a storeroom at the end of the counter.

"Get a mattress and two blankets in there."

The barred door to the right clicks open and the Professor, surrounded by three guards, walks into the bottom tier of 4A, past a row of cells on his left.

The slippers are too large, so the Wizard, carrying the mattress on his shoulders, is forced to shuffle as he passes the inspecting eyes of the prisoners, who begin to whoop and shout in pleased recognition.

"Hey! Whooee! Look who's here! Welcome to 4A, brother."

Dylan nods and smiles at the muscular blacks and stocky whites who stand by their bars, watching him stagger past. In the last cell of the row, a small man sits on the floor in the lotus position, smiling benevolently.

While the soul fuckers shot it out in San Francisco, the Castalia Foundation, a continent away in Millbrook, New York, was becoming a world-recognized center for research in consciousness extension and self-induced brain change. To the 64-room *Alte Haus* situated on an estate "twice five miles of fertile ground," came thousands of self-appointed messiahs, occultists and adepts. Millbrook was the Wimbledon of the spiritual upheaval. However simplistic, spaced-out, disorganized and anarchic this neurological phenomenon may have been, let no one doubt that the experiences were philosophically intense.

From 1963 to 1968, there were no acts of physical threat, muscular coercion or symbolic intimidation at Millbrook. Of spiritual banditry, however, there was an epidemic.

Dylan himself was scared witless scores of times by the energies released. At one peak of naivete, he took the innocent precaution of assuming that any wild-eyed pilgrim who knocked on the great oaken door waving celestial credentials should be admitted and given temporary benefit of doubt.

While the soul fuckers shot it out in San Francisco, the Castalia Foundation, a continent away in Millbrook, New York, was becoming a world-recognized center for research in consciousness extension and self-induced brain change.

After five years' experience, the Millbrook became quite sophisticated in reacting with sympathetic skepticism to this army of divinities.

When a stranger would announce, "I am a special agent of God!" the genial answer would be: "Welcome to the club. So what's new with you?"

A cell door opens to a small anteroom, which leads to a second door, beyond which is a dark windowless cave. The guards close both doors and the Alchemist finds himself in a strip cell in the Adjustment Center.

In it are a seatless toilet, chipped and stained, a rusty-metal face bowl and a metal slab on which he throws the soiled, smelly mattress. The room is dark except for a rectangle of light that comes through the outer door. He has 24 years left to serve.

The Philosopher feels a sense of elation. This is it, he thinks. The indisputable, undeniable, Dantean bottom. After 18 jails and prisons on four continents, this is the ultimate pit. Now that the death penalty has been abolished, a strip cell at the end of the row in the bottom tier of Folsom's 4A is the nadir. "From here begins the journey home," he says to himself, looking up.

> During the Indochina Wars, where the Western Imperial tide was thrown back, Americans took sides, and the two parties, Hawks and Doves, fought in the streets. It was at this moment that Dylan's brief political career temporarily distracted him from his role as Evolutionary Agent. With superhawk Nixon's ascension to power in 1968, the Evolutionary Agents were savagely repressed. Among those arrested—and, of course, convicted—was Agent Dylan. Aided by bands of red-larvals, he escaped the dungeons of the Past and fled to the Middle World, only to be imprisoned again by North African pirates. Such events were all too typical of that backward planet in primitive ages.

After ten minutes of darkness and silence, the outer door opens and a young blond prisoner enters. He leans against the bars of the inner door, smiling cheerfully.

I'm sorry you're here, man, but welcome. I'm the trusty for the first tier. Do you smoke?"

"Yeah. And is there anything to read?"

"Sure. What do you like? I bet you don't like shit kickers, right? I'll get you

Aided by bands of red-larvals, he escaped the dungeons of the West and fled to the Middle World, only to be imprisoned again by North African pirates. Such events were all too typical of that backward planet in primitive ages.

something good. You may not be down here too long. If they figure you're not violent, they'll move you upstairs."

The trusty slides out, leaving the outer door open. Reflected light of the setting sun warms the cell. In a few minutes, he is back, carrying a white envelope filled with tobacco, a pack of rolling papers and four paperbacks.

"These came from Charlie. He's in the next cell." That would be the guy sitting in the lotus position, looking benevolent. "He wants to know if you take sugar and cream with your coffee. And if you like honey."

"Sure. Anything," says the Neurologician, smiling.

The trusty grins and disappears.

> But as to what really happened in the Sixties while the Acid-Assassin Dylan and his cronies were at large, there was no general agreement. The whispered words "spiritual revolution" could be heard in college classrooms, collective-farm meetings, youth congresses, suburban *dachas* and hooligan radio broadcasts. The infamous Dylan seemed to be everywhere, instigating continuous thought-crime and neurological child molesting, until the socialist masses themselves demanded that the authorities confine him to an educational labor camp. A new outbreak of rumors—sexual, pornographic, extraterrestrial, involving multiple agents and convoluted espionage networks—spread further terror and an enigmatic eeriness.

Sitting on the bunk, Dylan sniffs at the tobacco. Bugler. He rolls a cigarette and watches the smoke puff and cloud in the sunlight.

Twenty-four years left to serve.

He examines the books that Charlie has sent via trusty. *The Teachings of the Compassionate Buddha. In Search of the Miraculous. The Teachings of Don Juan.* And *The Master and Margarita*, a thick paperback novel about life in modern Russia, by Bulgakov. Some improvement on the *Reader's Digest* condensed novels from previous holes.

Now the blond trusty is back bringing envelopes filled with sugar cubes and powdered cream, a cardboard cup filled with organic honey, a box of crackers.

"Charlie sent you these. I gotta go now. The bulls are watching me. I'll be back later if you need anything."

By the use of white magic—neurological techniques that enable people to understand and to control their own nervous systems—he neutralized occult power moves.

The disciplined study of advanced levels of consciousness and brain change inevitably leads to a consideration of black magic, which at Millbrook was defined as the use of neurological techniques to obtain power over others. Dylan decided at that time that he would have nothing to do with black magic and deliberately refused to learn anything about satanic rituals. He was operating on the tar-baby assumption that any admission of black magic into consciousness could contaminate and make one susceptible to it.

Later, after belatedly discovering that he was being hexed, vexed, perplexed, painted into pentagons, exposed to Kali death-goddess mantras and flashed by charms and jujus, he decided to learn enough about the dark arts to recognize and react—not so much for self-protection, but to defuse misguided practitioners. By the use of white magic—neurological techniques that enable people to understand and to control their own nervous systems—he neutralized occult power moves. He became adept at sensing precisely how realities are created at the beginning of an interaction, of how realities are subsequently imposed on others and of how reality invasions can be checked. He developed dozens of simple, humorous and aesthetic protections against black-magic reality take-overs.

One example is the Buddhist mudra—or hand movement—which means "have no fear." The thumb and index finger are joined to form a circle; the three remaining fingers are extended, as in the American OK sign. The circle thus formed can be used to focus consciousness. Through the circle, one sights the person who is projecting an unwanted reality. Then one shifts focus to one's own hand, and the person splits into two peripheral fuzzy optical blobs. And one's attention is centered on one's own ability to maneuver and control one's own consciousness.

Thus, years earlier, did Dylan prepare for his first-and-only reality skirmish with Charles Manson, who began by imposing a reality in which he came on as Biblical prophet.

The prisoner sits on the floor, looks over the cell again. Reduced to isolation and helplessness, the bio-survival circuitry and emotional-glandular systems react in primitive, emergency patterns. The trained Neurologician scans the circuitry, turns off the surrender/bail-out/die reflex, tunes in the success/bliss/patience networks and serenely waits for the past to catch up with the future. Eighteen prisons and jails in five years are good preliminary training in neurological engineering.

"This is eternity, brother. This is the end of the line. No one ever gets out once they've been here. This is forever."

He hears a voice.

"So you finally made it here. I've been watching you fall for years, man. You know where we are?" The voice is cocky, somewhat patronizing. The lotus-position character in the next cell, who sent the books and coffee makings. Charlie. He repeats: "Do you *really* know where we are?"

"Where are we?"

"This is eternity, brother. This is the end of the line. No one ever gets out once they've been here. This is forever."

Dylan listens to the voice with pity and irritation. He senses that Charlie speaks a resigned subjective truth. True, that is, for Charlie. The Commodore is not willing to be included in that reality, which he is planning to discard. But anybody on the inside deserves compassion. Besides, the Neurologician understands how this reality has been formed. Fear is the force that energizes and structures our social institutions, and Charlie is the totally institutionalized man, a Kafkaesque symbol of our technical-moral domestication. The military mind.

"Hey," Dylan calls. "Did you send me the Bugler and the food? Thanks."

"It's my pleasure," says the voice. "I love everyone and try to share what I have. I've been waiting to talk to you for years. Our lives would never have crossed outside. But now we have plenty of time. We were all your students, you know." The voice is low with the assurance of a fundamentalist minister.

"What do you mean?" The Wizard is leaning against the bars, cocking his ear to catch the soft, self-assured words.

"You know how it happened. I had been in prison all my life, and when I got out in the middle of the Sixties, there was a whole new world. Millions of kids cut loose from the old lies, free of hangups, waiting to be told what to do." The voice takes on a slight edge of complaint. "And you didn't tell them what to do. That's what I never could figure out about you, man. You showed everyone how to create a new head and then you wouldn't give them the new head. Why didn't you? I've wanted to ask you that for years."

"That was exactly the point," the Professor replies wearily. "I didn't want to impose my realities. The idea is that everybody takes responsibility for hir nervous system, creates hir own new reality. It's the end of the monotheism trip, remember. You can be anyone this time around. Anything else is brainwashing."

"That was your mistake," the voice says in a ghost-hollow whisper.

"That was exactly the point," the Professor replies wearily. "I didn't want to impose my realities. The idea is that everybody takes responsibility for hir nervous system, creates hir own new reality."

"Nobody wants responsibility. They want to be told what to do, what to believe, what's really true and really real."

"And you've got the answers for them?"

"It's all in the Bible, man. That's the one thing prison does for you. Gives you time to read the Bible. I figured it all out. Do you know why everything went wrong?"

The bard remembers: He is the guest, the receiver of gifts—little gifts, but all Manson could give. Patiently, he asks, "Why?"

"It was the women. They got scared and forced all these laws and morals on the men. It's all in the Bible, man. What does the Bible say about women? That they're the cause of evil. Right? Don't you get the message? Read it while you're here. It's ruthless and stern. Evil has to be killed. Only a few are to be saved. I'm the only one who really takes the Bible seriously and that's why I'm here."

The Professor asks quietly, "How do you feel, Charlie?"

There is a pause and then the voice returns, less messiah, more convict.

"I feel bad, man." After the confession, a new rush of words: "I got the rawest deal in two thousand years. Sure I laugh at it most of the time. But the pigs got me good. I can't write letters. I can't get visits. They got me completely cut off. They really want to kill me. I can feel it. The murder in their hearts. My trial was a farce. It's stupid. I play out *their* script, act out *their* Bible, take the whole thing on myself—all *their* feelings of evil and murder, all the sins of mankind, climb on the cross for them. And nobody understands. Nobody sees what I'm doing for them. Do you? Like do you understand about Sirhan Sirhan?"

The Psychologist answers carefully: "I recognize that this is a very Christian country and that every convict is forced to play Christ. But, to tell you the truth, I don't have much to do with that. I'm an Irish-Celtic pagan. Oldest god game going."

Manson should not be feared, lest he be made fearful. Dylan's feelings toward his fellow prisoner were pitying and he certainly had no desire to wish the unfortunate fellow further harm.

Later on, in the yard of Folsom, he would fall into a conversation with Bob Hyde, a wild, tough, wise veteran of the prison system.

"Why is Manson locked in segregation?" asked the Commodore.

"He'd get beat up if he came out on the yard. Not because of what he did

The Professor eats dinner on the floor. It is passed through a swine trough on a plastic tray and eaten with plastic spoons too fragile to be used as weapons. As he eats, he watches the light from the hall throw a yellow puddle on the floor.

on the street. That ain't important in here. Prisoners can't act as judges for each other. We take a man as he comes. Manson's first problem in prison and on the street is his size. He's a runt, you know. Can't be over five-two.

"Now, if he was six-two and two hundred pounds, you better believe that he'd be walking around cheerful and confident, instead of sitting in lockup. Not that size is everything in prison. The Mexican Mafia is the most feared gang in the system, because it's organized and ruthless. Manson isn't accepted here because he's a head fucker—coming on with all that Bible talk. That may scare the squares out there, but in here, it don't cut it. Manson's conned himself into believing his own Bible trip."

The Professor eats dinner on the floor. It is passed through a swine trough on a plastic tray and eaten with plastic spoons too fragile to be used as weapons. As he eats, he watches the light from the hall throw a yellow puddle on the floor.

> Americans have eaten 1.8×10^{10} McDonald's hamburgers and elected Richard Nixon twice. We live at the bottom of a 40-mile gravity well. It has taken all four and a half billion years of terrestrial evolution to produce nervous systems capable of devising a technology with which to climb out of that well and launch migratory-colonization cylinders into space. There is no reason for us to ever climb back down into such a planetary hole again. Our evolutionary mission is to fly free through timespace. The original sin of "Genesis" is gravity: the fall.

The trusty is back. "Doc?"

"Yes?"

"What are the most important books in the world?"

"That depends. What do you want to learn?"

"About life. About metaphysics. About the higher life."

The Professor's tone is dry, pedantic. "Metaphysics means beyond physics. Do you know a lot about physics?"

"No. I'm not interested in science. I want to know about spiritual things."

"Well, you can't go *beyond* physics until you understand the basic principles of physics. Do you know what Einstein did?"

"He made the bomb."

"He showed mathematically that all matter is energy at different rates of speed. Think about that for a minute."

"Read all the books you can get about the future. And leaving planet earth. And finding immortality. And contacting higher intelligence."

"It's far-out, yeah. But I want to know about God. Do you believe in astrology? Do you believe in the tarot? Charlie keeps telling me to read the Bible. My cellmate has the *I Ching*. It's heavy, man; 740 pages. Should I read the Bible or the *I Ching* first?"

"Don't bother with either of them. They're thousands of years out of date."

"Well, what *should* I read?"

Long pause. Sirag, Wheeler and Sarfatti on new quantum theories? Paul on non-histone proteins? Ettinger and Harrington on longevity? O'Neill on extraterrestrial migration? Sagan on contacting advanced civilizations in space?

"Read science fiction."

"What? That's not spiritual."

"Yes, it is. Read all the books you can get about the future. And leaving planet earth. And finding immortality. And contacting higher intelligence."

After the trusty leaves, the Bard's eyes tire rapidly and he abandons, for the night, Bulgakov's satire on a robot society where the free mind is chained, caged, confined. Sleep comes quickly.

BUGLIOSI: Directing your attention to verse 15, which reads: "And the four angels were loosed, which were prepared for an hour, and a day, and a month, and a year, for to slay the third part of men." Did he (Manson) say what that meant?

WATKINS: He said that those were the people who would die in Helter Skelter . . . one third of mankind . . . the white race.

After breakfast, Charlie's voice is there again.

"Hey, I want to ask you a question. Are you there? Are you listening?"

"Yes, I'm listening."

"When you take acid. And the world and your body dissolve into nothing but vibrations. And space becomes time and there's nothing but pure energy, nothing to hang onto. You know what I'm talking about?"

"Yes."

"Well, that's the moment of truth, right? But what is it? What do *you* call it?"

The ultimate Cosmological question posed. A silence ensues in the cell block of the maximum-security prison, broken only by the humming of a

Death is obsolete, or will be soon. They laid that trip on you, Charles, and you bought it. I'm really sorry because that moment is just the suspension of biochemical imprints in the nervous system."

generator, the clunk of toilet valves, the sound of rushing water, a distant rattling of metal keys.

"Charles?"

"Yeah?"

"What do *you* find at that moment?"

"Nothing. Like what death must be. Right? Isn't that what you find?"

"Death is obsolete, or will be soon. They laid that trip on you, Charles, and you bought it. I'm really sorry because that moment is just the suspension of biochemical imprints in the nervous system. You can take off from there and go anywhere you want. You should have looked for the energy fusion that's called love."

> Later, from the perspective of post-terrestrial migration, Dylan would send back the message to Manson and his followers: S.M.I.²L.E., or, in larval language, Space Migration, Intelligence Increase, Life Extension. "They need something to S.M.I.²L.E. about," the Commodore would say.

Footsteps and jaunty whistling in the hallway. The young blond trusty leans in.

"Hey—home! You're getting moved. Just heard the bulls talking. You're going up to the third level."

"What does that mean?"

"It's good. You're going up. You're getting out of the hole in the hole."

The Philosopher folds the tobacco, sugar, coffee, honey and the four books in blankets, throws the mattress onto his shoulder and, surrounded by the three clubs, leaves the strip cell, walks back down the tier past the hard-core cells. Charlie Manson, sitting in the lotus position, smiles and waves.

The power of terrorists to frighten the middle class was dramatized to Dylan in a later conversation with a young and inexperienced guard. A group of convicts was in the prison dayroom watching the documentary film *Manson*, produced by Robert Hendrickson. It contains a scene in which Brenda, flanked by other Manson girls, idly toys with a rifle, looks directly into the camera and quietly says, "We are what you have made us. We were brought up watching *Gunsmoke, Have Gun Will Travel, FBI, Combat—Combat* was my favorite show. I never missed *Combat*."

The Philosopher throws the mattress on his shoulder and, surrounded by the three clubs, walks back down the tier past the hard-core cells. Charles Manson, sitting in the lotus position, smiles and waves.

At this point, the young guard rushed in the dayroom in an agitated state.

"Who was saying that?" he demanded.

"A girl from the Manson family."

"That's the scariest thing I ever heard in my life."

"Yeah, the continual violence on TV is alarming," agreed the Commodore. "The daily body count on this TV set alone runs into the hundreds."

"No, I don't mean that," said the guard. "I mean Manson and those girls, threatening us that way. I want to run home and put double locks on my doors."

"But that girl says that they are just acting out the popular TV scripts and the Bible's instructions to get rid of sinners."

"Well, I'm glad I got a couple of rifles and a bunch of pistols in my house."

"And the TV antenna on your roof to receive the programs that tell you what to be afraid of."

"That stuff is weird," said the bewildered guard.

Dylan nodded in agreement.

A Minor Intelligence Affair

March 1976
San Diego Federal Prison

Commodore Tom Dylan walked into the office of the Senate Committee on Subversive Activities and nodded cheerfully to Klute, the Chief Investigator, a burly bi-ped earthling with the tweed-demeanor of a College Dean.

Klute rose and approached Dylan with a happy smile. The two embraced and shook hands—chuckling and reciting the standard affectionate welcome noises exchanged by terrestrials who trust each other.

The Chief Investigator introduced his three deputies, alert looking primates who greeted the Commodore with respectful smiles. **Shoulder holsters. C.I.A. or F.B.I.?**, thought Dylan. **The vibes are good.**

"Coffee, Commodore? Let's see, you take everything, as I recall," said Klute.

The door opened silently and an attractive black female earthling entered the room carrying a tray with steaming cups and a plate of doughnuts.

Dylan and two of the deputies lit nicotine cigarettes.

Klute cleared his throat.

The tape is running, thought Dylan. **That's good. The Director and the Senators will get it direct.**

"We wonder if you would be willing to answer some questions which the committee is really concerned about."

"With pleasure. That's my job," replied the Commodore, who, after all these years, had finally mastered the social habits of the bureaucrats.

The Chief Investigator introduced his three deputies, alert looking primates who greeted the Commodore with respectful smiles. "Shoulder holsters. C.I.A. or F.B.I.?," thought Dylan. "The vibes are good."

"We still don't understand what happened in the late 60s and 70s," said Klute, stuffing tobacco into his pipe, frowning with his serious young man look. "This militant revolutionary stuff. What caused upper-middle class kids, affluent and well educated to embrace political violence? The Weather Underground. The S.L.A. Why?"

Here we go again, thought the Commodore. **They just won't quit.** "Of course you want to show foreign influence," said Dylan. "Moscow, Peiping, Hanoi and Havana must be to blame for these alien influences, correct?"

The four agents exchanged uneasy glances. Everyone suddenly lifted coffee cups. Cigarette smoke filled the room. Everyone shifted position.

"That's what we're told," replied the Chief Investigator, choosing his words carefully. "What other explanation is there for this sudden explosion of revolutionary aggression? European Marxists don't act so violently. So we need your help. You've traveled the third world. You've lived with these people. What countries? What foreign agents? What contacts?"

"My role in these matters is not blind transmission of information," said the Commodore stiffly. **Why are they interested in foreign influence now? Why now? That stuff won't get appropriations anymore.** "Present me with a problem that requires intelligent synthesis of historical facts and I'll solve it for you. I'm really more interested in the history of your species than you, as you are well aware. I'm always fascinated by what your people define as a problem."

"I know," said Klute somberly but smiling. "Our questions are your data. So here's your question. Was there any tie between the Weathermen and Communist countries while you were in Algeria?"

The Commodore leaned back in his chair and laughed. **This is going to be amusing.** "First let me retrieve the factoid memories." He closed his eyes during the neural scan. "Okay. Delegations of American leftists did visit China, North Korea, North Vietnam. Think of them as naive pilgrims to the shrines of their gullibility. Spiritual tourists. Like Catholics from South Boston visiting Lourdes. Plus, of course, your planted agents who heavily infiltrated the delegations. In Algeria all visiting leftists made obligatory visits to the North Vietnamese embassy and were given those horrid, heavy steel rings with the inscription FLN-SVN . . . the rings made from metal salvaged from downed American planes."

The agents' eyes flicked at each other. **Ah**, thought Dylan, **that was the plus-fact they needed to show my cooperation. Now they'll probe with an obvious minus-fact.**

Why are they interested in foreign influence now? Why now? That stuff won't get appropriations anymore.

"What about Bernadine Dohrn's secret visits to Algeria?" from Klute stuffing his pipe.

"It was so secret that I never heard of it. There were, however, certain other Americans secretly negotiating to end the war on terms totally favorable to the enemy. Do you want their names?"

The four agents leaned forward in unison. "We sure do."

"Kissinger and Nixon," replied the Commodore. "Do you really think that Hanoi was interested in directing sporadic Weather bombings of R.O.T.C. buildings at the same time they were winning their poker game with Kissinger? If I had wanted to escalate the Vietnam war I would have infiltrated Weather and provoked them to senseless militancy. Neither Hanoi or the American left understood the groundswell cultural revolution that ended the war and threw Johnson and Nixon out of office. Nor, apparently do your people."

"Tell us what we don't understand," replied Klute dryly.

"With pleasure. Please tell the Senators and the Director that they are continuing to repeat the same mistake that Hoover, Johnson and Nixon made. You can blame domestic unrest on outside agitators and Moscow gold—in order to get your Congressional appropriations. But the mistake is to believe your own lying. You recall that Johnson fell because he clung to the belief that opposition to his war must be based on foreign agents. And then Nixon fell for the same propaganda. The Watergate burglars were hoping to find evidence of Castro payments to Larry O'Brien. If they had found checks from Fidel in the Democratic Headquarters the burglars would have been heroes and Watergate a glorious patriotic success. Right?"

The four agents sat hunched in the standard pose of cops being scolded by a superior. It was Klute who broke the silence. "You still haven't answered our question. Who turned the middle class kids onto violence?"

"I can tell you who. And how your guys set it up."

The Chief Investigator and the three deputies leaned forward, pens poised over yellow legal note pads.

"Who did it?" whispered Klute.

"Your own lower class steeped in violence and hip to the ghetto-fact that middle-class security is based on the violence of their protectors—the police and the military. The kids off the block, the ex-cons, black and white, to whom the gun and the fist have always been the basic equalizers. The well ordered society maintains educational control over its young by keeping the

"It's good that we can talk this openly," thought Dylan. "That means that the young guys control the tapes made in this office."

children of the managers away from the unsettling raw facts of power politics. Your guys made a great blunder by throwing middle-class kids in prisons for victimless, cultural crimes like draft resistance and dope. Prisons, as you well know, are schools for violence where you teach lower class kids how to play their roles as criminals. Middle class kids are supposed to read about social problems in college text books. They aren't supposed to be exposed to the true facts about the crime industry."

The Chief Investigator wrote rapidly with a black felt pen. The three deputies sat in cautious silence.

"What about the Marxist rhetoric and the Castro revolutionary slogans?" said Klute wearily.

"Your college kids read Fanon and Che and Marighella on urban guerilla tactics. They drooled over that stupid movie **Battle of Algiers**. All this was standard parlor intellectual stuff until Johnson and Nixon made the tactical mistake. Was it a mistake? Or was it a deliberate tactic?"

"What mistake?"

"Throwing the verbally aggressive college kids into close contact with lower class muscular violence. The bourgeois kids taught the ghetto kids the rhetoric. Suddenly every rapist and armed robber became a political prisoner. And the college kids learned the emotional power of the gun and the fist to create fear and respect."

"Why do you ask if this was a tactic?" asked Klute.

He's good, thought the Commodore. **He knows all this. He's just getting me to say what he wants said. His faction in the bureau is using me as conceptual hit-man to roll the heads of the old guard.** The Commodore had long ago learned that the worst enemy of any police-bureaucrat was the faction in his own department that wanted his power. And that criminals and crime waves were created by competing factions among powerholders.

"Well, Nixon and Reagan rode into power on the wave of fear generated by the student uprisings. I'm glad to help clarify this issue. But I sure hope you know what you're doing."

"What do you mean?" asked Klute, smiling. **In relief?**

"We all know that there are powerful people in the government who don't want these things said. They're going down, sure, but they aren't going down meekly. And there are, I suspect, lots of indictable records stuck away in the files that haven't been shredded. Can you protect me if I front for you?"

The four agents looked at each other and began to laugh. "Yes," said Klute. "You're safe. As safe as we are."

"Who turned the middle class kids onto violence?"
"I can tell you who. And how your guys set it up."

The four agents lauged again. "We've gone so far out on a limb to rescue you that you can advocate anything except high-jacking and we'll protect you. The facts of the matter are that if you go down, we'll go down with you."

"That's what Cleaver said in Algeria," replied the Commodore soberly. "I told him, as I now tell you, that I'm more interested in us all going up." **It's good that we can talk this openly,** thought Dylan. **That means that the young guys control the tapes made in this office.**

"We agree," said Klute rising from his chair. "And right now let's all go to lunch."

At the restaurant the agents seemed relaxed and cheerful. **I must have given them what they wanted,** thought Dylan. He turned his head and smiled into the eyes of Klute.

"You guys aren't still chasing dissidents are you?"

Klute looked at his colleagues and they all laughed.

"Shall we brief the Commodore?" said Klute.

The agents nodded, smiling grimly.

"No we aren't chasing leftists. In the first place, we've so infiltrated every left group that the **Berkeley Barb, Rolling Stone** and the **New Republic** would fold in a day if we pulled out our people.

"Since McCord and Judge Sirica started this Watergate business no police agency in Washington will touch a left-wing case. Don't you hear what is obsessing every federal agency these days?

"The return of the avenging Democrats."

The four agents glanced at each other and nodded.

"You realize who the worst enemy of the Director of any agency is?" demanded Klute.

"The rival political faction in his own agency," replied Dylan promptly.

"For sure. Now tell me who is the worst enemy, the dangerous security threat to the head of the F.B.I. office in Topeka, Kansas."

"The head of the F.B.I. office in Kansas City," replied Dylan.

"Exactly," said Klute. "And who are the other threats to the chief in Topeka?"

"The local sheriff, the local police chief, the local narcotics agency."

"Affirmative. And are the local Mafia and the local Black Panthers and the local Communists threats to the F.B.I. chief?"

"No, they are pawns to be used or avoided according to bureaucratic developments."

"Affirmative," said Klute. "Now tell me, as the Watergate scandal develops what is every Federal Agency Director doing?"

"He's good," thought the Commodore. "He knows all this. He's just getting me to say what he wants said. His faction in the bureau is using me as conceptual hit-man to roll the heads of the old guard."

"Covering tracks, covering up illegal or partisan political acts, shredding memos in anticipation of November 1976 when rival factions in each agency move in to expose what's been going on since 1968."

"Right. So you can be certain of one thing," said Klute. "The central concern of every Federal Law Enforcement bureaucrat these days is to avoid prosecution in 1977. You, of all people, should know how many "dirty tricks" and political crimes were committed by Nixon."

"And by Johnson," agreed the Commodore.

"And by the Kennedys," added Klute. "Take your kidnapping in Afghanistan by American agents. The officials who stole your passport and had you shipped back under armed guard are, right now, wondering if they'll face a forcible abduction charge when a liberal, pro-marijuana president gets elected in 1976."

"About the Kennedys," said the Commodore, "I figure their crimes and dirty tricks haven't surfaced because they weren't as pious and hypocritical as Nixon."

"They never hid their criminal past," murmured Klute, "people respected that instinctively."

"And they're dead," added Dylan.

"Some people still wonder who killed them," mused the Inspector.

"Do you know?" exclaimed the short Deputy Inspector.

"Sure I know," said Klute breezily. "And the Commodore knows too."

Dylan nodded smiling.

"Who killed the Kennedys?" asked the Deputy Inspector.

"They were killed by their own device," said Dylan.

"The Kennedys," Klute added quickly, "were killed by the crashing of the complicated structure they temporarily destroyed, the ricochets of the bullets they fired."

"What structure?" asked the Deputy Sheriff.

"The code of honor among the thieves and assassins who run almost every government in the world."

"That's right," added Dylan. "Among every Mafia group there's a code of self-protective ethics. Generals wine and dine captured generals for obvious selfish reasons. And Sicilians may kill rivals but they never touch each other's families. The IRA bombs Protestant kids but don't torture. The Arab Mafia and the Jewish Mafia each have their own codes."

"What does this have to do with the Kennedys?" asked the Deputy.

"The Kennedys," Klute added quickly, "were killed by the crashing of complicated structure they temporarily destroyed, the ricochets of the bullets they fired."

"The Kennedys broke the rule that governs the game of government leaders," said Klute.

"And it was so karmically reckless," said Dylan, "that business about the three pairs of brothers was so obvious."

"Three pairs of brothers?"

"Don't you remember. At one time there were two sets of brothers who ran the two countries which pre-occupied the gang warfare plans of the Kennedys."

"Fidel and Raoul Castro, and . . . ?"

"The Diem brothers in Vietnam. You remember what happened."

The deputy whistled softly. "Jack and Bobby sponsored all those plots to kill Fidel."

"And they set up the Big Minh coup that assassinated the Diems." said Klute. "It was barbarian Borgia duplicity imposed by the two Big Brothers on a world that had been mildly civilized since Hitler and Stalin. Even Kooky Stalin was canny enough not to sponsor assassination plots."

"Because," said the Commodore, "once a Mafia moral taboo is broken, every one gets into the act."

"And no capo is safe."

"I see now," said the deputy, "why no one is eager to uncover the Kennedy scandal. Too many agencies involved in the assassination plots. Will any of this ever come out?"

"That's the point of your visit, isn't it?" asked Dylan. "It's all going to come down after the 1976 elections. (Lots of blood on honest cops' hands and lots of burglar tools in honest cops' pockets.)"

"And all in the name of national security."

"So the question of foreign support of domestic dissidents could save some high level heads?" said Dylan. "By the way, when, if ever, will I know the results of this meeting?"

Klute shrugged his shoulders and made his little-boy gesture of contrived ignorance. "Who knows? These matters have a way of getting leaked to the press at the right time. You should know that, Commodore."

"Yes, I'm aware of how images are made and changed by press leaks," said Commodore Dylan. "I wish you guys luck. I hope you know what you're doing."

"We'll all find out soon enough," replied Klute.

Two months later, the Commodore received in the mail an unmarked envelope which contained the xerox copy of an article in the New York *Times*:

"But one source familiar with the prosecutors' thinking said today that reliable information from high sources assured the Security Committee that the Weather Underground had no foreign connections."

NO FOREIGN LINKS TO FUGITIVES SEEN
U.S. Prosecutors Discount Alien Threats
in Targets of Federal Agency Burglaries.

Washington Aug. 22—

Justice department prosecutors have seen no evidence that the Senate Security Agency's search for fugitive members of the Weather Underground organization was motivated by the group's purported links to hostile foreign governments, sources close to the department's investigation said today.

The issue of whether the fugitive group had been directed or supported by foreigners has been raised by Murray Steinmetz, an attorney for some 20 Senate Security agents who have become subjects of a Justice Department investigation into burglaries they carried out against friends and relatives of the fugitives over the last five years.

Mr. Steinmetz asserted last week that such connections had existed between the Weather fugitives and "foreign hostile governments" and other Washington sources have said that the Senate Committee is attempting to marshal evidence of those links as a prelude to demonstrating that the break-ins were legal.

But one source familiar with the prosecutor's thinking said today that none of the Security Committee documents requesting or granting permission for the burglaries had suggested or even alluded to such foreign connections to the Weather Underground as rationale for their commission.

The Washington *Post* reported today that the Senate Committee on Security was preparing a 500-page report showing that some of the Weather fugitives received financial support from the Vietnamese and Cuban governments. The newspaper quoted a "high justice department source" who cited concern that such evidence could weaken the department's criminal case against the agents.

Two sources close to the prosecutors dismissed the suggestion that there was such a concern. "It's too late," one said, "The dam has burst." And another noted that several past and present federal agents had already accepted immunity from prosecution in return for their testimony about the burglaries.

From Outer World to Inner World
To Inner Space to Outer Space

Co-Author
Robert Anton Wilson

February 1974
Vacaville Prison

The infamous Drug Revolution of the 1960s has inspired more nonsense, on both sides, than any event of our time.

It was not a sudden mutation from a society without drug use to a society with massive drug use. Far from it: America, before the 1960s, was a heavy, hard drug culture already, but the drugs widely used were not **defined** as drugs. They were "medicines" (aspirin, barbiturates, tranks, amphetamine "diet-pills," etc.) or "Relaxants" (tobacco, alcohol, caffeine).

The accompanying chart, from *Sex and Drugs* by Robert Anton Wilson (Falcon Press, 1987), gives the actual figures on drug use in the U.S.A. at the end of the 1960s, when the "Drug Revolution" was completing its first decade. It will easily be seen that, even at that late date, the most popular drugs in the country were not those usually associated with the "Drug Revolution" but those which had been around for generations. The

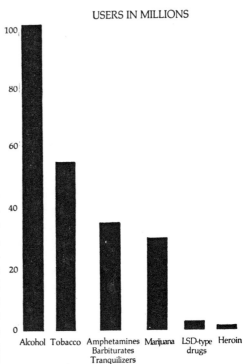

USERS IN MILLIONS

DRUGS IN PERSPECTIVE

" . . . we began to speak of the experimental subject as a neurological cosmonaut tripping through inner space, the session being programmed by a 'trip-guide' who acted as Ground Control."

acceptable tobacco, booze and pills were still the majority drugs; the forbidden weed, psychedelics and junk were still by comparison minority preferences. The acceptable drugs, the prescription drugs and (among the forbidden drugs) junk had not increased markedly in use. What had increased was the usage of psychedelic drugs.

The much-exaggerated chemical metamorphosis of our time has not been from no drugs to drugs, but **from one kind of drugs to another**.

To understand this is to begin to understand what has been happening. The change, we will show, has been from **mood-change** drugs to **brain-change** drugs. From **down** drugs to **up** drugs. From the earthy to the spacey, from gravity to levity, from low times to High Times. Psychedelic drugs are vehicles for exploring the brain.

These metaphors are not as extravagant as they seem. They are part of a new and meaningful slang that is heard everywhere from academia to the ghetto. For instance, the explorer metaphor began in the Harvard psychedelic research project of 1960-62, when we began to speak of the experimental subject as a neurological Columbus tripping through inner space, the session being programmed by a "trip-guide" who acted as Ground Control. This imagery is still subliminally carried along by the words **trip, tripping, tripper,** now in international use.

To understand neurological space, assume that the nervous system consists of eight potential circuits, or "gears," or mini-brains. Four of these brains (including the left lobe) are concerned with our social survival; four are post-terrestrial, reside in the "silent" light lobe, and are for use in our future evolution. The light lobe usually inactive at early stages of our development, can be activated when the person ingests psychedelics.

We will explain each of the 8 "brains" briefly.

I. The bio-survival circuit. This marine or vegetative brain was the first to evolve (billion years ago) and is the first activated at birth. It programs perception onto an either-or grid divided into nurturing-helpful Things (which it approaches) and noxious-dangerous Things (which it flees, or attacks). The imprinting of this circuit sets up the basic attitude of trust or suspicion which will last for life. It also identifies the external stimuli which will ever after trigger approach or avoidance.

II. The emotional circuit. This second, more advanced bio-computer emerged when vertebrates appeared and began to compete for territory (perhaps 500,000,000 B.C.). In the individual, it is activated when the DNA mastertape triggers the metamorphosis from crawling to walking. As every

The imprinting of the first three circuits determines by age 3½ the basic degree and style of trust/distrust, assertiveness/submission and cleverness/clumsiness with which the mind will handle tools or ideas.

parent knows, the toddler is no longer a passive (bio-vegetative) infant but a mammalian politician, full of physical (and emotional) territorial demands, quick to meddle in family business and decision-making. Again the first imprint on this circuit remains constant for life (unless brain-washed) and identifies the stimuli which automatically trigger dominant, aggressive behavior or submissive, cooperative behavior. When we say that a person is behaving emotionally, egotistically or "like a two-year-old," we mean that SHe is blindly following one of the robot imprints on this circuit.

III. **The dexterity-symbolism circuit.** This third brain emerged when neolithic hominid types began to differentiate from other primate stock (circa 4-5 million B.C.) and is activated in the individual when the older child begins handling artifacts and sending/receiving laryngeal signals (human speech units). If the environment is stimulating to the third circuit, the child takes a "bright" imprint and becomes dextrous and articulate; if the environment is made of deliberately stupid people, the child takes a "dumb" imprint, i.e. remains more or less at a 5-year-old stage of symbol-blindness.

In popular speech, the first brain is generally called "consciousness" per se: the sense of being biologically alive, in this body, oriented to the survival of the body. (When you are "un-conscious," the first circuit is anesthetized and doctors may perform surgery on you or enemies may attack, and you will not evade them or flee.) The second circuit, in the same vernacular language, is called "ego." So-called "ego" is the second circuit mammalian sense of status (importance-unimportance) in the pack or tribe. The third circuit is what we generally call "mind"—the capacity to receive, integrate and transmit signals produced by the hominid hand (artifacts) or the hominid 9 laryngeal muscles (speech).

The imprinting of these three circuits determines, by about age 3½, the basic degree and style of trust/distrust that will color "consciousness," the degree and style of assertiveness/submissiveness that will determine "ego"-status, and the degree and style of cleverness/clumsiness with which "mind" will handle tools or ideas.

In evolutionary terms, first brain "consciousness" is basically invertebrate, passively floating toward nurture and retreating from danger. Second brain "ego" is mammalian, always struggling for status in the tribal pecking-order. Third brain "mind" is hominid, hooked into human culture and dealing with life through a matrix of human-made gadgets and human-created symbolism.

The fourth brain is post-hominid, specifically characteristic of **Homo Sapiens**, the "domesticated" person in industrial society. This is:

IV. **The socio-sexual circuit.** This fourth brain was formed when hominid

The first four circuits are called "terrestrial" because they have evolved in and have been shaped by the gravitational, climatic and energy conditions determining survival of gene-pools on this sort of planet.

packs evolved into societies and programmed specific sex-roles for their members, circa 30,000 B.C. In the individual it is activated at puberty, when DNA signals trigger the glandular release of sexual neurochemicals and the metamorphosis to adulthood begins. The first orgasms or mating experiences imprint a characteristic sex-role which, again, is bio-chemically bonded and remains constant for life, unless some form of brain-washing or chemical re-imprinting is accomplished.

In daily speech, fourth circuit imprints and programs are known as the "adult personality," the domesticated sexual impersonation.

Masters and Johnson have demonstrated that specific sexual "dysfunctions"—so-called "perversions," "fetishes," low-or-no performance conditions like premature ejaculation, impotence, frigidity, etc., or eccentric imprints defined as "sinful" by the local tribe—are determined by specific experiences in early adolescent mating. The same is true of the equally robotic behavior of the "normal," "well-adjusted" person. The sex-role (or, as it might more appropriately be called, the **sexual impersonation style**) of the human is almost as rote and repetitious as that of other mammals (or birds or fishes or insects).

These four circuits are normally the only networks of the brain activated. It should now be clear why we call them terrestrial. They have evolved on, and have been shaped by, the gravitational, climatic and energy conditions determining survival and reproduction of gene-pools on this kind of planet circling this variety of Type G star. Intelligent individuals evolving in space, not living at the bottom of a 4000-mile well, not competing for territory on a finite planet-surface, not limited by the forward-back, up-down, right-left parameters of earthy life, would inevitably develop different circuits, imprinted differently, not so inflexibly Euclidean.

Forward-back is the basic binary choice programmed by the bio-computer operating on Circuit I: Either advance, go forward, sniff it, touch it, taste it, bite it—or retreat, back away, flee, escape.

Up-down, the basic gravitational sense, appears in all ethological reports of animal combat. Rear up, swell the body to maximum size, growl, howl, shriek—or cringe, drop the tail between the legs, murmur softly, skulk away, crawl and shrink the body size. These are domination and submission, fight-flight signals common to iguana, dog, bird, and the Chairman of the Board of the local bank. These reflexes make up Circuit II "ego."

Right-left is basic to the polarity of body-design on the planetface. Right-hand dominance, and associated preference for the linear left-lobe functions of the brain, determine our normal modes of artifact-manufacture and conceptual

To activate the first brain take an opiate. To activate the second brain take alcohol. To activate the third brain take an energizer.

thought, i.e. third circuit "mind." Asymmetry is the key to improved brain function.

It is no accident, then, that our logic (and our computer-design) follows the either/or, binary structure of these circuits. Nor is it an accident that our geometry, until the last century, has been Euclidean. Euclid's geometry, Aristotle's logic and Newton's physics are meta-programs synthesizing and generalizing first brain forward-back, second brain up-down and third brain right-left programs.

The fourth brain, dealing with the transmission of tribal or ethnic culture across generations, introduces the fourth dimension, time—binding cultures.

Since each of these circuits consists of bio-chemical imprints or matrices or digital blueprints in the nervous system, each of them is specifically triggered by neuro-transmitters, i.e. drugs.

To activate* the first brain take an opiate. Mother Opium and Sister Morphine bring you down to cellular intelligence, bio-survival passivity, the floating consciousness of the newborn. (This is why Freudians identify opiate addiction with the desire to return to infancy.)

To activate the second brain, take an abundant quantity of alcohol. Vertebrate territorial patterns and mammalian emotional politics immediately appear when the booze flows, as Thomas Nashe intuitively realized when he characterized the various alcohol states by animal labels: "ass drunk," "goat drunk," "swine drunk," "bear drunk," etc.

To activate the third brain, try coffee or tea, a high protein diet, speed or cocaine.

The specific neurotransmitter for circuit four has not been synthesized yet, but it is generated by the glands after pubescense and flows volcanically through the bloodstreams of adolescents.

None of these gene-pool designer drugs changes basic neuro-chemical imprints. The imprints which they trigger are those which were wired into the nervous system during the first stages of imprint vulnerability. The Circuit II drunk exhibits the emotional games or cons learned from parents in infancy. The Circuit III "mind," under speed or coke, never gets beyond the permutations of those artifacts and symbols originally imprinted, or abstractions associated with the imprints through later conditioning. And so forth.

But all this Pavlovian-Skinnerian robotism changes drastically and dramatically when we turn to the right-lobe, the future circuits and extra-terrestrial chemicals.

The four evolving future "brains" are:

V. The Cyber-Somatic circuit. When this fifth "body-brain" is activated, flat

---

* Most probably, this "activation" results from a general **suppression** of higher neural circuits which leaves the cerebral brain dormant.

About 20,000 years ago, the specific fifth brain neurotransmitter was discovered by shamans in Asia and quickly spread throughout Europe and Asia. It is, of course, cannabis.

Euclidean figure-ground configurations explode multi-dimensionally. Gestalts shift, in McLuhan's terms, from linear **visual space** to all-encompassing **sensory space**. A hedonic **turn-on** occurs, a rapturous amusement, a detachment from the compulsive mechanisms of the first four circuits.

This fifth brain began to appear about 4000 years ago in the first leisure class civilizations and has been increasing statistically in recent centuries (even before the Drug Revolution), a fact demonstrated by the hedonic art of Egypt, India, China, Rome and other affluent societies. More recently, Ornstein and his school have suggested with electro-encephalograms that this circuit represents the first jump from the linear left-lobe of the brain to the analogical right-lobe.

The opening and imprinting of this circuit has been the preoccupation of "technicians of the occult"—tantric shamans and hatha yogis. While the fifth circuit imprint can be achieved by sensory deprivation, social isolation, physiological stress or severe shock (ceremonial terror tactics, as practiced by such rascal-gurus as Don Juan Matus or Aleister Crowley), it has traditionally been reserved to the pagan-primitives and to the educated aristocracy of leisure societies who have solved the four terrestrial survival problems.

About 4,000 years ago, the specific fifth brain neurotransmitter was discovered by shamans in the Caspian Sea area of Asia and quickly spread to other wizards throughout Eurasia and Africa. It is, of course, cannabis.

It is no accident that the cannabis-user generally refers to his neural state as "high" or "spaced-out." The transcendence of gravitational, linear, either-or, Aristotelian, Newtonian, Euclidean, planetary orientations (Circuits I-IV) is, in evolutionary perspective, part of our neurological preparation for the inevitable migration from gene-pools and off the home planet, now beginning. This is why so many pot-heads are **Star Trek** freaks and Sci-Fi adepts. (Berkeley, California, certainly the Cannabis Capital of the U.S., had a Federation Trading Post on Telegraph Avenue, where the well-heeled could easily spend $500 or more in a single day, buying **Star Trek** novels, magazines, newsletters, bumper stickers, photographs, posters, tapes, etc., including even complete blueprints for the **Starship Enterprise**.) Hedonic Consumerism.

The extra-terrestrial meaning of being "high" is confirmed by astronauts themselves. Most of those who have entered the free-fall of zero gravity describe "mystic experiences" or rapture states typical of the neurosomatic circuit. "No photo can show how beautiful Earth looked," raves Captain Ed Mitchell, describing his Illumination in free-fall. He sounds like any successful yogi or psychedelic hipper. No camera can show this experience because it is inside the nervous system.

The mammalian politics which monitor power struggles among terrestrial humanity are transcended, in this info-world . . . One is neither coercively manipulated into another's territorial reality nor forced to struggle against it with reciprocal emotional game-playing.

(Captain Mitchell left N.A.S.A. to found The Institute of Noetic Sciences, concerned with scientific research into right-lobe functions. Buzz Aldrin has joined him.)

Free fall, at the proper evolutionary time, triggers the neurosomatic mutation, which has previously been achieved "artificially" by yogic or shamanic training or by the fifth circuit stimulant, cannabis. Surfing, skiing, skin-diving and the new sexual culture (sensuous massage, vibrators, imported Tantric arts, etc.) have evolved at the same time as part of the hedonic conquest of gravity. The Turn On state is always described as "floating," or, in the Zen metaphor, "one foot above the ground."

VI. The Cyber-Electronic Circuit. The sixth brain consists of **the nervous system becoming aware of itself** apart from imprinted gene-pool reality-maps (circuits I-IV) and even apart from body rapture (circuit V). Count Korzybski, the semanticist, called this state "consciousness of abstracting." Dr. John Lilly calls it "meta-programing," i.e. awareness of programing one's programing. This Einsteinian, relativistic contelligence (conscious-intelligence) recognizes, for instance, that the Euclidean, Newtonian and Aristotelian reality-maps are just three among billions of possible quantum programs or models for experience.

This level of brain-functioning seems to have been reported first around 500 B.C. among various "occult" groups connected by the Silk Route (China-North India). It is so far beyond the gene-pool circuits that those who have achieved it can barely communicate about it in ordinary language (circuits I-IV) and can hardly be understood even by fifth circuit Rapture Engineers.

The characteristics of the Cyber-Electric circuit are high velocity, multiple choice, relativity, and the ability to program and reprogram the brain.

The gene-pool politics which monitor power struggles among terrestrial humanity are transcended in this info-world, i.e. seen as static, artificial charades. One is neither coercively manipulated into another's territorial reality nor forced to struggle against it with reciprocal emotional game-playing (the usual soap-opera dramatics). One simply elects, consciously, whether or not to share the other's reality-tunnel.

Tactics for opening and imprinting the sixth circuit are described and rarely experienced in advanced rajah yoga, and in the hermetic (coded) manuals of the medieval-Renaissance alchemists and Illuminati.

No specific sixth circuit chemical is yet available, but strong psychedelics like mescaline (from the "sacred cactus," peyote), psilocybin (from the Mexican "magic mushroom," tonactl) and LSD open the nervous system to a mixed-media

---

THINK FOR YOURSELF   ESCAPE THE GENE POOLS

The Einstein revolution in physics, breakthroughs in quantum psychology, cybernetics and neurology, the synergetic language of Buckminster Fuller, the Neurologic of Lilly & Leary, allow us to describe sixth circuit functioning as the nervous system serially re-imprinting itself.

---

series of Circuit V and Circuit VI channels. This is appropriately called "tripping," as distinguished from straightforward fifth circuit "turning on" or "getting high."

The opening of the sixth circuit is so alarming to gene-pool circuit I-IV expectations that it has been traditionally described in paradoxical, almost nonsensical metaphors. The Not-Self. The No-Mind. The White Light of the Void.

This semantic surrealism is no longer necessary. The Einstein revolution in physics, the quantum psychological breakthroughs in cybernetics and neurology, the synergetic language of Buckminster Fuller, the Neurologic of Lilly and Leary, computer linguistics, allow us to describe sixth circuit functioning in operational and functional terms as the nervous system metaprogramming the nervous system or serially re-imprinting itself.

The suppression of scientific research in this area has had the inevitable result of turning the outlaw drug culture back toward fifth circuit hedonics and pre-scientific models of right-lobe experience. (The occult revival.) Without scientific discipline and methodology, few can successfully decode the often-frightening (but philosophically crucial) sixth circuit metaprogramming signals. Those scientists who continue to study this subject dare not publish their results (which are illegal). They record their findings only in secret notebooks—like the scholars of the inquisitorial era. (Voltaire announced the Age of Reason two centuries too soon. We are still in the Dark Ages.) Many underground alchemists have given up on such challenging and risky self-work and restrict their trips to body-hedonics, i.e. fifth circuit cannabis raptures.

The evolutionary function of the sixth circuit is to enable us to communicate in Einsteinian relativities and neuroelectric accelerations, not using third circuit laryngeal manual symbols but directly via feedback, telepathy and computer link-up. Neuro-electric signals will increasingly replace "speech" (hominid grunts) as personal computers become standard home appliances.

When humans have climbed out of the atmosphere-gravity well of planetary life, left the gene-pool, accelerated 6th Circuit contelligence will make possible high-energy communication with "higher Intelligences," i.e. ourselves-in-the-future and other post-terrestrial races.

Think of it like this: the higher right-lobe circuits (V-VIII) raise to higher consciousness and other time-dimensions on the corresponding, more primitive left-lobe circuits (I-IV). Thus, Circuit V centers on the same body-centered sensory-somatic loops as Circuit I; but Circuit V is time-expanded, "laid-back," funny, hedonic, **conscious**, where Circuit I, bonded to survival, is instantaneous, reflexive, blind, robotic. Similarly, Circuits II and VI both deal with "politics." Circuit II, however, only allows us to bargain or bluster for freedom-or-

---

Circuit VII is best considered, in terms of 1976 science, as the genetic blue-print archives activated by anti-histone proteins. The DNA memory bank coiling back to the beginning of life.

submission with those on the same evolutionary level (our own species) or downward to species below us but using the same proxemic-kinesic body-language (dogs, cats, etc.) Circuit VI allows us to engage in reality-brokering with species above us in evolution, i.e., the more advanced intelligences of the galaxy.

It is charmingly obvious, once we realize that spaced-out neural experiences really are post gene-pool and post-terrestrial, that "getting high" and "spacing out" are accurate metaphors. Circuit V neurosomatic rapture is preparation for the next step in our evolution, migration off the planet. Circuit VI is preparation for the step after that, interspecies communication with advanced entities using **electronic** (post-verbal) reality-maps.

Circuit VI is the "universal translator" often imagined by sci-fi writers, ROM programs already built into our brains by the DNA tape, just as the the behavior algorithms of the future butterfly are already built into the caterpillar.

VII. The Cyber-Genetic Circuit. The seventh brain kicks into action when the nervous system begins to receive signals from **within the individual neuron**, from the DNA-RNA dialogue. The first to achieve this mutation spoke of "memories of past lives," "reincarnation," "immortality," etc. That these adepts were recording something real is indicated by the fact that many of them (especially Hindus and Sufis) gave marvelously accurate poetic vistas of evolution 1000 or 2000 years before Darwin, and foresaw Superhumanity before Nietzsche.

The "akashic records" of Theosophy, the "collective unconscious" of Jung, the "phylogenetic unconscious" of Grof and Ring, are three modern metaphors for this circuit. These visions of past and future evolution described by those who have had "out-of-body" experiences during close-to-death episodes also describe Circuit VII contelligence.

Specific exercises to trigger Circuit VII are not to be found in yogic teaching; it usually happens, if at all, after several years of the kind of advanced rajah yoga that develops Circuit VI facility.

The specific Circuit VII neurotransmitter is LSD. (Peyote and psilocybin can produce Circuit VII experiences also.)

Circuit VII is best considered, in terms of 1976 science, as the genetic blue-print archives, activated by anti-histone proteins. The DNA memory coiling back to the dawn of life. A sense of the inevitability of immortality and interspecies symbiosis comes to all Circuit VII mutants; we can now see that this, also, is an evolutionary forecast.

Genetic consciousness alerts us to the possibility of extended longevity leading to immortality.

Here, for example, are 23 alternatives to passive, belly-up submission when your Blue Cross runs out.

The word "death" is changed to "Involuntary, Irreversible Metabolic Coma." Here, for instance are 23 alternatives to passive belly-up submission when your Blue Cross runs out.

I. PSYCHOLOGICAL/BEHAVIORAL TRAINING TECHNIQUES FOR LIFE EXTENSION

1. Meditation & hypnosis
2. Carefully Designed Psychedelic Drug Experiences of "Dying" and genetic Consciousness.
3. Experimental Out-of-Body Experiences using Ketamine.
4. Sensory Deprivation/Isolation Methods
5. Re-programming exercises (suspending the effects of and replacing early "death" imprints imposed by culture.
6. Development of New Rituals To Guide the Post-Body Transition (Creation of Hibernation Clubs, people who band together to facilitate Hibernation)
7. Pre-Incarnation Exercises (Using Altered-State methods to imprint future scripts)
8. Aesthetically-orchestrated Voluntary "Dying": Control of one's Hibernation (Suicide)

II. SOMATIC TECHNIQUES FOR LIFE EXTENSION

Techniques to inhibit the process of aging comprise:
9. Diet: Consult the classic work on diet-longevity by Roy Walford, M.D.
10. Life Extension Drugs
11. Exercise Regimes
12. Temperature Control
13. Sleep Treatments (hibernation)
14. Immunization to counter aging

III. SOMATIC/NEURAL/GENETIC PRESERVATION

15. Cryonics or Vacuum-pack (pickling)
16. Cryonic Preservation of Brain and/or DNA
17. Cellular/DNA Repair
18. Cloning
19. Cybernetic (Post-Biological) Methods for Attaining immortality:
20. Archival-Informational Relicts
21. Head Coach: Personality Data Base Transmission
22. Nano-tech Information Storage: Direct Brain-Computer Transfer at the atomic level
23. Computer Viral: Persistence in Gibson's Cyberspace Matrix

Self-reproducing nanocomputers could be grown with manyfold the power of today's super-computers of a size small enough to reside within biological cells! Organic life can thus be created!

VIII: The Cyber-Atomic Stage

So far we have defined seven obvious stages of human evolution which operate at our current primitive state of knowledge. This book outlines the neuropolitical systems which these stages produce:

1. Bio-survival is the assignment of the . . . Trib-al society.
2. Political Power is the obsession of the . . . Feud-al society.
3. Manufacture-dexterity produces the factory mechanisms of the . . . Industri-al society.
4. Disciplined conformity of electronic media produces the . . . Imperi-al society.

(The next stages are post-political. Only individuals can attain these levels.)

5. Hedonic-artistry produces the . . . Sensu-al-Aesthetic Individual.
6. Electronic-computer facility produces the . . . Cybernetic Individual of the Information Age.
7. DNA engineering produces the . . . Cyber-Genetic Individual.

—NOW we have one very hot informational skill just (1988) becoming available—

8. Nanotechniques produce the . . . Neuro-Atomic Person, the Singularity.

The prefix "nano" refers to a quantity of a billionth. A nanometer is a millionth of a millimeter. This is the order of a wavelength of light! Sober, serious scientists are today researching "nanoengineering," the construction of mechanical devices at the atomic scale.

It is theoretically possible (and thus probable to build tiny tools made up of the smallest components available in the universe: molecule by molecule. Nano tools are "molecular assemblers" which work like conventional DNA or RNA in acquiring the correct components to the growing structure.

We are talking about "atom-stacking," cyber-atomic artist-design. It involves the use of atoms as tools and carriers of thought.

As the size of any mechanical or muscular device decreases, its speed can increase. The wings of insects beat faster than those of a hummingbird. Due to their tiny scale, the molecular assembler tools, like tiny robots with an arm made of several hundred atoms and a programmed instruction set, would move millions of time per second resulting in the very rapid construction of conventional-sized assemblages. Self-reproducing nanocomputers could be grown with manyfold the power of today's super-computers of a size small enough to reside within biological cells!

Organic life can thus be created!

So what does this have to do with the subject matter of this book: Neuropolitics? What social form does the Nanotech Age produce?

The first four gene-pool circuits contain the learned lessons of our evolutionary past (and present). The post-gene-pool self-directed circuits are the evolutionary script for our future.

Only the Gods know. Because Atomic Engineering will provide our species all of the technologies and mental skills usually attributed to . . . ourselves in the future.

The Gods.

In Gods We Trust.

We suggest that Circuit VIII deals with the universe as it is—an information program of "bits" which flash off/on in accordance with basic algorithsm—**infra, supra** and **meta**-physiological. A quantum mechanical communication system which does not require a biological container. The attempt to construct a quantum model of consciousness and/or a conscious model of quantum mechanics by such turned-on physicists as Prof. John Archibald Wheeler, Saul-Paul Sirag, Dr. Jack Sarfatti, etc. indicates strongly that the "atomic consciousness" first suggested by Leary in "The Politics of Ecstasy" (1962) is the explanatory link which will unite parapsychology and paraphysics into the first scientific empirical experimental theology in history.

When the nervous system is turned on to this quantum-level circuit, time-space is obliterated. Einstein's speed-of-light barrier is transcended; in Dr. Sarfatti's metaphor, we "escape electro-magnetic chauvinism." The contelligence within the quantum projection booth **is** the entire cosmic "brain," just as the micro-miniaturized DNA helix **is** the local brain guiding planetary evolution. As Lao-Tse said from his own Circuit VIII perspective, "the greatest is within the smallest."

This neuro-atomic contelligence is four mutations beyond terrestrial domesticity. (The Reagan Drug Wars [1980-1988] are between Circuit IV tribal moralists-or-collectivists and Circuit V hedonic individualists.) With our need for higher intelligence, richer involvement in the cosmic script, further transcendence will no longer be satisfied by physical bodies, not even by immortal bodies capable of genetic engineering, Circuit VIII will open a further frontier. New universes and realities. "Beyond theology: the science and art of Godmanship," as Alan Watts once wrote.

It is possible that the mysterious "entities" (angels and extra-terrestrials) monotonously reported by Circuit VIII visionaries are members of races already evolved to this level. Even more exciting is the theory propounded by Saul-Paul Sirag, based on Godel's mathematics, that They are ourselves-in-the-future.

The first four gene-pool circuits contain the learned lessons of our evolutionary past (and present). The post-gene-pool self-directed circuits are the evolutionary script for our future.

"... The finer part of humanity will, in all likelihood, never perish—they will migrate from sun to sun as they go out. And so there is no end to life, to intelligence and to the perfection of humanity. Its progress is everlasting."

The neurogenetic meaning of the cultural revolution is now clear. The Cyber-chemicals, psychedelic drugs, are designed to be pursuitist, not escapist. They open the nervous system to the possibilities of future post-terrestrial evolution. And they reaffirm the interstellar optimism of aero-space pioneer and sci-fi prophet Konstantin Tsiolkovsky who foresaw and designed prototypes for much of the technology of the 1970s, 1980s and 1990s as early as 1910 and 1920. As Tsiolkovsky wrote, "The murky view which some scientists advocate as to the inevitable end of every living thing on Earth . . . should not now be regarded as axiomatic. The finer part of humanity will, in all likelihood, never perish—they will migrate from sun to sun as they go out. And so there is no end to life, to intelligence and to the perfection of humanity. Its progress is everlasting."

The Sexual Domestication
of the Four-Brained Biped

Author
Robert Anton Wilson

November 1973
Casa Arlena
Berkeley, CA

Frank, the Hip San Francisco Disc Jockey, has finally cajoled his luscious wife (played by Marilyn Chambers, the Ivory Soap advertising angel) to join him on the swinging Bay Area orgy circuit. Remember? 1973? **The Resurrection of Eve**, the most elegantly arty (and frequently revived) porn epic to date? One panting-gasping-bongo-orchestrated reel too late, Frank is aghast by Eve's suddenly awakened passions, especially for black young males with jumbo-sized prongs, "The way it used to be . . . " he starts to complain. And she tells him all. Everything. What's really coming down. The straight scoop from Evolutionary Central, in just three little words: **"It's over Frank."** As the film ends, porn has at last achieved a typical European static-ambiguity ending (right out of Polanski's **Knife in the Water**, in fact).

And Marilyn-Eve, fresh from her baptismal cleansing in 99 and 44/100ths pure Ivory, a true witch-initiate, spells out the next evolutionary mutation. The "search for the apocalyptical orgasm" has triumphed—the search which Mailer alone in "The White Negro" (1958) had defined as the vector of the Hip Revolution, before anybody else realized there **was** a Hip Revolution. Sexual Armageddon has arrived. We don't need Steinem to tell us that the Patriarchal Age is over. We don't need Alvin Toffler to remind us that the nuclear family has been fissioned along with the atom itself. We only need to look around to see that we are in the midst of the greatest bio-social upheaval since the Neolithic Revolution founded cities, created centralized government and **domesticated** humanity.

Sexuality (along with every aspect of our culture) will be transformed more in the next thirty years than in the previous thirty thousand.

We are in the primitive, larval stages of the mutation. The chief cause of our accelerated changing, changing, changing, is the extension of our nervous systems through chemistry and technology (as Buckminster Fuller and Marshall McLuhan keep reminding us). Our culture is dramatically influenced by the fact that there are more scientists alive and engaged in research today than in all previous generations added together. **Sexuality** (along with every aspect of our culture) **will be transformed more in the next thirty years than in the previous thirty thousand.** (We will be mutating from gene-pool terrestrials to post-terrestrial singularity, for instance, much more rapidly than most people realize.)

Scan the socio-sexual trends—remember that all this is overture, preamble:

The United States divorce rate is now almost 50 percent (and over 75 percent in California, the most **avant** segment of the union). The remarriage rate among the divorced is a fantastic **80 percent**. These two facts mean that the U.S., the most advanced technological nation on the planet and the harbinger of change, **de facto** has evolved from a culture of traditional monogamy to one of consecutive marriage or serial polygamy. This is about as major a cultural change from frontier mores as if we had switched from Christianity to Islam.

Acceptance of pre-marital sex is no longer a minority or heretic stance. A clear majority of students in both a middle-class and a lower-class San Francisco high school, in a recent study, approve of what used to nervously be called "going all the way." (Exact figures were 53 percent of the males and 58 percent of the females in the middle class school; 64 percent of the males and 48 percent of the females in the lower class school.) Paul C. Glick, senior demographer at the Census Bureau's population division, reports that cohabitation outside marriage increased **800 percent** during the 1960s. Illegitimacy increased 200 percent since the 1950s.

Other census figures show the number of new marriages falling and new divorces rising faster in 1975 than during the previous tumultuous decade. (Divorce stood at 2.2 per thousand in 1960, reached 2.5 in 1965, 3.5 in 1970, and is now over 4.6.) In New York State, the divorce rate jumped 300 percent between 1969 and 1975.

While communes, group marriages, crash pads, come and go, form, reform, break-out, start anew, no very exact figures on this retribalization are available, but the nuclear family is clearly evolving. A recent United Press study of 22 cities showed that in 54 percent of them, marriage license bureaus reported dramatic decreases in new marriages. In San Francisco, the drop was over 25 percent in five years.

To see sex realistically (for once), try seeing it as part of the evolution of the nervous system.

Women are having more pre- and extra-marital sex than ever before. Six out of ten teen-age mothers are now unwed or got married about the time of giving birth. While male infidelity remains where Kinsey found it in the 1940s (around 50 percent), female extra-marital affairs have increased from about 25 percent to 40 percent; and this breaking out of the monogamy game is occurring earlier (average age 40 in Kinsey's sample; average age 35 today). 50 percent of the wives in Bell's latest study predicted that they "certainly" or "possibly" would have affairs in the future. This trend is strongest in the youngest (as always); in Kinsey's females, only 8 percent had been unfaithful to their husbands by age 24; now it is 24 percent.

And in the **Redbook** study of last year, 40 percent of a large statistical sample (100,000 wives) complain that they are not having **enough** sex. Let us call this the "Resurrection of Eve" syndrome. It portends apocalypse in every bedroom.

Marijuana, used by only one or two hundred thousand (mostly Southern Blacks and Mexican-Americans) when Congress outlawed it in 1937, is now— on the eve of decriminalization—used by somewhere between 30 and 40 million. A great deal of this Weed-smoking has erotic meanings, in several dimensions, as Barbara Lewis demonstrated at length in **The Sexual Powers of Marijuana**, and as antipot crusaders enviously suspected all along. 85 percent of the grass-smokers interviewed by Prof. McGlothlin in a 1968 study mentioned enhancement or stimulation of sex as one of their main reasons for using the heavily-penalized cannabis in preference to the legal anti-aphrodisiac alcohol.

The hipster search for the transcendental Maileresque or Reichian orgasm is not only the root of all this ferment but the beginning of the de-domestication of sex. Conservatives, of course, have been more aware of this, in their own suspicious way, then optimistic liberals and academic humanists. A whole phase of human civilization is ending. Nietzsche and Aleister Crowley saw moral (i.e. sexual) apocalypse clearly at the dawn of the 20th Century and celebrated the collapse of domesticity (inaccurately) as the re-birth of heroic barbarism— Nietzsche's "blonde beast" warrior-Superman, Crowley's self-identification as the Great Beast in **Revelations** whose law was "Do what thou wilt." Alas, both of these bards of evolution were better at analyzing what was dying-off than at discerning what was actually being born.

To see sex realistically (for once), try seeing it as part of the evolution of the nervous system. Mailer correctly identified the hip quest for erotic transmutation as part of the hipster's "attempt to build a new nervous system." The extensions of our nervous systems, our self-created scientific sensors, are all exploding. The speed of communications increased 10^7 times since 1900, and is accelerating

None of our social organizations are prepared to deal with change. Utopianism, Futurism, Science Fiction are the only realistic "politics" around these days.

faster in this decade. Speed of travel in the same period is up 10^2, data processing 10^6 and known energy sources 10^3. "UnWoManned" spaceships have reached other planets.

Prof. J.R. Platt of the University of Michigan, who made these calculations, comments ominously that **"None of our social organizations are prepared to deal with change on such a scale."** Utopianism, Futurism, Science Fiction are the only realistic "politics" around these days. The mammalian Left and reptilian Right are both obsolete, blind, irrelevant. None of our social organizations can house the new humanity being born. We are literally, demographically, too big for the womb-cultures which nourished us.

The loosening of monogamous robotry has followed inevitably the rise of contraceptive effectiveness from 50-70 percent (douches and old-fashioned condoms) to 98-99 percent (the coil, the pill). The inevitable advance to 100 percent perfect contraception can be no further away than 1985. Pregnancy outside the womb will be common by 1990, completing the biological liberation of women and ensuring their political liberation. Genetic engineering means that longevity can't be much further away—and some of the brightest young scientists in that field, such as Paul Segall of Berkeley, aree already aiming beyond longevity for immortality. O'Neill's space-cities, housing not monastic astronauts but families, tribes, human communities, will circle the sun, beginning the greatest evolutionary mutation since the ascent from the ocean to land.

We can now see that the domestication of humanity was a necessary but temporary stage.

The mammalian (and other animal) nervous system evolves in metamorphic stages, over long historical spans, **and this is quickly recapitulated and imprinted for local conditions in each individual.** Imprinting is a bio-chemical process in which certain pathways, patterns, networks are bonded in synergetic response-units, activated to trigger the same robot-reaction whenever similar events happen in the environment. Ethologists have demonstrated that conditioning can only build further associations onto the basic bio-chemical imprint. Conditioning cannot change or reverse imprint. The imprint stays in the neurons until it is changed bio-chemically. In most cases it stays until death.

The first circuit, formed in the evolution of the (marine) nervous system, and the first activated in each newborn human, is the bio-survival brain. This hooks the organism onto a maternal object and then slowly builds up a safe space of territory around her. This basic viscerotonic consciousness, being here-now, the DNA memory becoming identified with this nervous system in this small,

The sexual imprint literally freezes behavior into robot patterns almost as inflexible as the so-called "instinctive" mating rituals of birds and insects.

helpless body, in this social grouping, now. Basic feelings of anxiety or security are set by this imprint, and never change (unless bio-chemical re-imprint is achieved by careful scientific or brutal brainwashing techniques). In popular speech, this is the "will."

The second circuit evolved later in evolution (amphibian, post-marine), and deals with territory and status. As soon as the infant is able to walk, master gravity, exert muscular effort, and meddle in family politics (decision-making), the basic imprint is laid down. This is the emotional script, the tribal status, the sense of being strong-dominant-manipulative or weak-submissive-manipulated. In traditional language, this is the "ego."

The third circuit evolved in early hominid society and deals with artifacts, from the flint-axe to the Orion starship, and with verbalization (laryngeal signals), from "Me Tarzan, You Jane" to "E = mc^2." The basic imprint is made by age 3 and is either "bright-dexterous" or "stupid-clumsy." (Headstart programs failed because they started too late. Subsequent conditioning never reverses a basic bio-chemical imprint.) This circuit is usually called the "mind."

These circuits are designed by the DNA master-blueprint for the survival of the individual organism.

The fourth circuit provides for the continuity of the species. This circuit connects the sexual apparatus to an imprinted social behavior syndrome. The first orgasms or mating experiences create the bio-chemical imprint—in the human class of life, the sexual "role." Again, no amount of Behavior Mod or conditioning has ever shown any significant or consistent success in altering this basic bio-chemical imprint. This sexual impersonation is generally called the adult "personality."

The sexual imprint literally freezes behavior into robot patterns almost as inflexible as the so-called "instinctive" mating rituals of birds and insects. **Explicit male superiority, garter-belts, booze, black lace panties, cool jazz** defines one human imprint group as rigidly as any twig-gathering pattern defines the ritual of any robin or sparrow. **Attempted equality, long-hair, incense, grass, sleeping bags, Rock 'n' Roll** defines another imprint group just as rigidly.

The division of labor and the wide varieties of cultural style, together with **the astonishing ability of the nervous system to imprint almost anything**, prevent domesticated humans from realizing that their socialized sex-roles are just as rote as those of the ant and the platypus.

A fifth neural circuit has been emerging for at least a few thousand years. It has given rise to a great deal of mysticism, occultism, witchery and superstition, together with astonishing, sporadic breakthroughs in art, music, and science.

The fifth circuit of the brain defines "cybersomatic intelligence": the capacity to suspend, integrate, re-wire and hedonically engineer all the previous imprints in terms of direct, bodily sensation.

(There are also dawning sixth, seventh and eighth circuits, to be mentioned later.) The fifth circuit defines **cybersomatic intelligence:** the capacity to suspend, integrate, re-wire and hedonically engineer all the previous imprints in terms of direct, bodily sensation.

The first scientific study of this circuit, **Cosmic Consciousness,** by psychiatrist R.M. Bucke, proposed that this was a new evolutionary development, not a pathology, and seemed to be statistically increasing in recent centuries. Psychologist A.H. Maslow showed in **The Peak Experience** that this circuit appeared spontaneously in many cases, but only among "self-actualizing" (i.e. relatively undomesticated) individuals. More recently, Ornstein and his school have demonstrated that fifth circuit experiences are mediated through the right lobe of the brain, whereas circuits I-IV are mediated through the left lobe and lower brain centers.

Fifth circuit right-lobe experience is more or less familiar to:

a. Casual, recreational users of neurotransmitter chemicals, such as weed, who have mild-to-major fifth circuit raptures some of the times they turn on;

b. Scientific and shamanic technicians-of-the-nervous-system who have learned how to use such chemicals to re-imprint for Rapture Control, i.e. precise neurosomatic intelligence;

c. Other shamans and yogis who have learned how to turn on the rapture circuitry without ingesting biochemicals. This means producing similar bio-chemicals **within** the body, by various kinds of physiological stress. In yoga, this consists of what is now called "social deprivation." In most forms of shamanism, it consists of cheerfully scaring the student out of his wits until the ecstasy-chemicals typical of death or near-death are released to produce a re-infantile state and allow for a new imprint;

d. Some epileptics (e.g. Dostoevski) and schizophrenics (e.g. Van Gogh) have occasionally triggered bio-chemical mutations to fifth circuit rapture.

e. Tantra. An excruciatingly sensual art in which sexual fusion is prolonged until a neural electric-storm ("the rising of the serpent") triggers the neurosomatic mutation.

This cybersomatic fifth circuit is "polymorphous-perverse" in Freud's dismal Teutonic jargon; "childish, playful, creative," in Taoist descriptions; "just like ordinary life, but one foot above the ground" in the famous Zen metaphor. In some highly-significant and prophetic modern slang, it is "high," "spaced-out," "trippy," "floating," "flying," "far fucking out." It is the new nervous system Mailer's 1958 hipsters were seeking, and their pursuit of apocalyptical orgasm was an intuitive sense of the pivotal role of **Tantra**

Fifth circuit experiences are mediated by the right lobe of the brain, whereas the four survival circuits are mediated through the left hemisphere and the brain stem.

(hedonic engineering) in this mutation to extra-terrestrial, post-domesticated evolutionary stages.

A grim warning against the fifth circuit, and a stirring defense of fourth circuit domestic robothood, has been presented by George Gilder in his melodramatic book, **Sexual Suicide**. Correctly sensing that recent explosions of Fifth Circuit rapture and the new age of freedom between the sexes poses an evolutionary competition for the four-circuited domesticated species, Gilder eloquently defends traditional gene-pool authorized sex-roles.

Among four-brained creatures, he says, "sex is bound to their deepest sources of energy, identity and emotion. Sex was the life source and cohesive impulse of a people, and their very character was deeply affected by how sexuality was sublimated and expressed, denied or attained." By comparison, among post-domestic fifth-brained hedonists, Gilder says "sex is devaluated and deformed"—i.e., individualized, de-robotized.

Gilder understands how second circuit ego-politics and third circuit competence were basic preliminaries to the development of fourth-circuit sex-role. Among four-brained humans, he says, "The boy's sexual identity is dependent on acts of exploration and initiative." (Second circuit courage, third circuit dexterity.) "Before he can return to a woman he must assert his manhood in action. The Zulu warrior had to kill a man, the Irish peasant had to build a house, the American man must find a job." (Just as robotically as the penguin must find a specially colored stone and bring it to his mate.) "This," says Gilder, "is for them the classic myth and the mundane reality of masculinity, the low comedy and high tragedy of mankind." Or of mammalkind or antkind.

"Female historians are different," says Gilder, still identifying humanity with the four-circuit domesticated species and assigning women an insectile housekeeping role. We turn in relief to sci-fi prophet Robert Heinlein, who with relaxed precision suggests the multi-role flexibility of the post-gene-pool, post-domestic, post-terrestrial:

> A human being should be able to change a diaper, plan an invasion, butcher a hog, design a building, conn a ship, write a sonnet, balance accounts, build a wall, set a bone, comfort the dying, take orders, give orders, cooperate, act alone, solve equations, analyze a new problem, pitch manure, program a computer, cook a tasty meal, fight efficiently, die gallantly. Specialization is for insects.

The 110-billion cell human brain, including the Hedonic right lobe

Maoism is the highest, and ultimate, form of terrestrial domesticated four-brained humanity.

---

unactivated in domesticated primates, is designed to handle all these sex-role programs, and a million more; and to learn to reprogram itself for ever-higher intelligence, emotional stability and artistic-ecstatic meta-programming of its own programs.

Continuing his lonely struggle for domesticity, Gilder says, "Of all society's institutions that work this civilizing effect"—domestication—"marriage is perhaps the most important . . . The family is the only agency that can be depended on to induce enduring changes in its members' character and commitment." We shall ignore the curious ambiguity of the phrase "enduring change" and simply add that the family is the only agency before Chinese Communism, to be precise, for Maoism is a philosophy of total hive-domesticity.

The sexual roles imprinted on the adolescent four-brained human Gilder calls "the sexual constitution" of the tribe. This constitution, he shrewdly notes, "will deeply influence the productivity and order of the community." (Hive solidarity.) "It will determine whether social energies are short-circuited and dissipated or whether they are accumulated and applied to useful pursuits." **Useful** means useful to the gene-pool, the hive; **short-circuited** or **dissipated** energies are those which produce somatic pleasure, interpersonal fusion, brain reward, personal growth, individual freedom.

The Sexual Constitution (robot imprint), Gilder gushes, "will determine whether the society is a fabric of fully integrated citizens"—an ominous phrase—"or whether it is an unorganized flux with disconnected individuals pursuing sex and sustenance on the most limited and anti-social scale." What ominously Soviet semantics! The hive is all-virtuous; the free individual is, **by definition**, anti-social. **Pravda** would only improve Gilder's rhetoric by adding "decadent" and "hooligan" to the adjectives decrying the self-actualizing hedonic individual.

"A job is thus a central part of the sexual constitution," Gilder summarizes grandly. "It can affirm the masculine identity of its holder; it can make it possible for him to court women in a spirit of commitment; it can make it possible for him to be married and thereby integrated into a continuing community."

These blatantly insectile moral views cause Gilder to be equally alarmed by **all** fifth-circuit manifestations—**Playboy**, Rock and Roll, Women's Liberation, objective sexological scientists like Masters-Johnson, Gay Pride militants, hippies, liberal clergymen, anybody, literally anybody, who departs from the robot domestic imprint biochemically hooked into Gilder's neurons at puberty.

So-called "future shock" is, of course, actually present shock. **The present is the future of the nervous system**, in four-brained humanity, because the neurons

---

The DNA strategy calls for continuous acceleration of the genetic script, and evolution has never happened faster than at present.

normally do not take new imprints after the sex-role is fixed at adolescence. Nixon's sexual system was formed in 1925, Frank Sinatra's in 1930, etc. Thus, it only takes 10 years for a liberal to become a conservative, another 10 to become reactionary.

But Gilder is a valuable witness. He makes explicit the preoccupations of fourth-circuit hive humanity with gene-pool continuity as opposed to individual evolutionary exploration. The positive moral values for Gilder are "productivity," "fully integrated citizens" (hive units) and "social energies" (a curious phrase meaning individual energies preempted by the hive). The delightful Taoist-Einsteinian term "unorganized flux" becomes a sinful derogation to this stern moralist.

Maoism is the highest, and ultimate, form of terrestrial domesticated four-brained humanity. When a U.S. Embassy official admits ruefully that a woman can walk alone through a Chinese city at three in the morning, without danger, what American fourth-brained moralist is not envious, awed, secretly shamed? For the sake of evolutionary perspective, we have mildly satirized the domestic-social ethic, but we do not condemn it or despise it. "Women and Children to the life-boats first!" "Be ready to die for your tribe's survival!" "United We Stand!" "Defend Our Turf!" Out of such gallant mammalian politics the survival of the seed was ensured, the species continued.

It does become ominous when defenders of **status quo** domesticity—whether of the nuclear family or the Maoist collective—justify legislative and coercive force to prevent the emergence of higher levels of consciousness and evolution. The social moralist then becomes a neurological fascist relentlessly opposed to any conception of human destiny higher than docile ant-hill productivity.

What Gilder and all orthodox moralists fear is the unfolding of the fifth neurological-rapture circuit, freedom from static imprints, disciplined release of right-lobe ecstasy, the joyful experience of Zen freedom, the spirit of levity which will free individual atoms to float loose from the gene-pool molecule and form higher units in neurological (and physical) Outer Space.

It must be emphasized that the evolution from fourth-circuit gravity to fifth-circuit levity is much, much more than a struggle between generations. The DNA strategy calls for continuous acceleration of the genetic script, and evolution has never happened faster than at present. The bitterness of the old species grows increasingly paranoid, violent, vengeful.

Think of the short-lived but symptomatic Spiro Agnew cult. The random shooting of longhairs. The death-wish implicit in Gilder's grim title, **Sexual Suicide**.

There are no holds barred in the domesticate's genocide against the fifth-brain mutant. Pleasure is worse than treason.

The blockage, after many long years, of all attempts to secure justice in the Kent State youth-massacre.

Think of this: in all our years of reading book reviews, after assuming that we had by now witnessed every extreme of spiteful cruelty that critics can impose on creative artists, only once have we actually seen a reviewer express the wish to literally murder the subject of a biography. Was this a response to the history of some great scoundrel and mass murderer, some notorious thug or dictator, a Hitler, a Stalin, a Mao, a Nixon? No. It was a commentary upon a book about **Janis Joplin**—a long, hysterical diatribe against Janis, actually, with little comment on the book's own merits.

And this homicidal **berzerkersang** is historically important. The critic was (who else?) Midge Decter, one of the arbiters of New York lit-crit oligopoly, and the **New York Times** knew with intuitive precision that her polemic against Janis deserved a full spread over the first three pages. The middle-aged middle-class must have loved the review; it told them just what they wanted to hear. Many must have cheered aloud when Decter declared her instinctive impulse "to throttle her [Janis] on the spot."

Decter is direct and honest. She articulates without hypocrisy what must surely be the most fascinating phenomenon in genetic history, the genocidal hatred of one generation for its own children.

We are all bored with "generation gap" debate, but Decter will not let the issue die. Janis, she writes, "was proclaimed by a whole generation in our midst to represent their best and deepest impulses ... to know who Janis Joplin was is to know a good deal, if not indeed everything that matters about the epidemic of antic despair that carried off so many of our children in the late 1960s." Please re-read the last two sentences and remember this is not some Dallas-based Fundamentalist but the middle-brow intelligentsia.

"Epidemic" means some form of plague or disease that was, fortunately, destroyed by the Watergate crowd, the stop-and-frisk-laws, the no-knock laws, the bugs and wire-taps, the legions of terrorized D.E.A. informers, the curfews against young people, the Gestapoization of America under the Nixon counter-revolution. "Antic despair" refers to the cheerful, generous cultural revolution which, among other achievements, permanently changed and improved the student-teacher-administrator relationship in our universities, clarified the relationship between the sexes, liberated the body to healthy hedonism, imported a dozen varieties of Oriental neuro-science (and two dozen varieties of Oriental charlatanism) which spiced-up and enriched our epistemology and culture, provoked the ecology movement, recreated a true love for nature and

The caterpillar cannot understand the butterfly.

wild creatures, questioned the unquestioned careerist work ethic, ended the draft, stopped the war, spread the spirit of intelligent criticism so far that even Nixon, with the whole machinery of government beneath him, could not hold power once his crimes were published and documented.

"Carried off so many of our children" possibly refers to spiritual abduction. The "children" no longer buy the ethics, the politics, the aesthetics or the robot uniformity of Decter's generation.

Certainly Decter cannot refer to the physical casualties of Vietnam (50,000 dead on the American side), Kent State, Jackson State, the hundreds of thousands neurologically damaged or ruined by dope busts and imprisonment. Can Decter face the fact that her generation's anti-dope laws killed and warped more young lives than a century's worth of the most ignorant and irresponsible misuse of Weed ever could?

The crowning irony is Decter's naive belief that her generation has feasted deeply of the "true qualities of sexiness" while Joplin's undomesticated fans, and Joplin herself, had "only simulation of sex and all the other riches of grown-up experience."

Pity urges us to let that imbecility slide without comment. But apparently there are no holds barred in the domesticate's genocide against the fifth-brain mutant. Since the young are too kind and too sophisticated to get into debates with Decter about whose sex life is "richer," and since we are of the same age-group as Decter herself, let us say it once and for all. The erotic experiences of the fifth circuit, and of the 30-40 million young users of that fifth circuit stimulant, cannabis, are so varied, so uninhibited, so all-out far-out way-out intense, so artful, disciplined and stylish, so orientally rich and Tantrically ecstatic, so honest, so free of guilt and domesticated neuroses, so affectionate and tender, so merry and magnificent that they can be neither understood nor believed by Midge Decter.

The caterpillar cannot understand the butterfly.

After reading about Janis' alleged participation with Hell's Angels in what she calls an "unspeakable scene of degradation," Decter expresses her desire to murder this "incorrigible child." There speaks the authentic voice of the Grand Inquisitor. We should all be kinder and more loving with each other, in this period of evolutionary metamorphosis, but if we cannot manage that much generosity of spirit, we at least have the duty to respect the mysterious individuality of others. You don't have to like Janis Joplin's sexual imprint, Ms. Decter, anymore than she would have liked yours; but the desire to kill those who differ is the root of fascism.

Civilization, as Freud dismally admitted, is based on authoritarian State-control over individual life and individual sexuality.

Decter gloats that Janis died after "no more than a moment's enthusiasm." But millions of us live on a little warmer and shinier because Her radiation touched us. And the energy still moves the machinery of the "Janis Industry." The record companies, who separated Her from **Big Brother**, still prosper off Her sound. Royalties are paid to Her biographers. Decter gets three pages up front in the **Times** Book Section to perform necro-sadism upon Her corpse. We hope this paragraph would compensate Her a little for Decter's brutality. It's a small act of gratitude to Janis. Her eyes would smile thanks and She'd hand us the bottle of Southern Comfort. Is it worse to shoot heroin with Janis than shoot heroines with Midge?

(This is not old history, by the way. The prisons are still full of sensitive young nervous systems, post-larval, open and vulnerable, but lacking the neurological know-how to deal with the violence of the moralists. They are there for the same reasons that Janis' corpse is dug up and savaged by Decter: for no crime against life or limb, no theft or swindle, but the manifestation of cultural dissent.)

Civilization, as Freud dismally admitted, is based on authoritarian State-control over individual life and individual sexuality. Domestication, the fourth-brained stage of evolution, is, in fact, (as Freud also realized in his own jargon) "the sublimation and repression of Eros," the creation of Gilder's "social energy" out of the robotic submission of the masses. Monogamous marriage, the Mom-Dad form of child-rearing, although necessary to the fourth-brained stage of development, has mostly been a neurological and genetic trial of passage.

Domesticated robot-sex, as every sane person from Ibsen to Gloria Steinem has realized, is a socially-acceptable form of prostitution. He gives Her $$$$$. She gives Him a tepid orgasm. "Frigid fucking for Frigidaires," as poet Kenneth Rexroth said so bitterly.

Most of the men who go to prostitutes, according to Judge Murtagh's sane and compassionate book, **Cast The First Stone**, are married. Domesticates who are theoretically "getting their sex" from a female domesticated robot at home. What are they paying extra money for, to a stranger? The truth is funnier and more tragic than any satire. Harmless frivolities like fellatio, in almost all cases. Simple hedonic arts that their robot-mates did not imprint in uptight Christian culture and are too senile (at 25 or 35) to learn. A minority of johns, of course, are seeking fetish-relief—satisfaction of "bizarre" imprints which, statistically, just happen because of the vulnerability of the nervous system to imprint anything at the sensitive moments of adolescence. [Written in 1973]

The attempt to **eroticize marriage** has spawned the enormous industry of sex-manuals, sensitivity sessions, cosmetics, costumes, erotic reconditioning

The attempt to eroticize marriage has spawned the enormous industry of sex-manuals designed to free robots enough to cure their more obvious inhibitions. It can't work. You cannot recondition until you re-imprint.

stimuli designed to free the robots enough to cure their more obvious miseries. It can't work. **You cannot recondition until you re-imprint.** The fifth-circuit chemical, cannabis, has changed more sex compulsions than all the reconditioners and retrainers in the world—but at the cost of setting the post-larvals more free than the gene-pool will tolerate.

It is imperative to understand that no anthropological study of "primitive" tribal groups has found the prevalence of neurosis, hysteria, rape, violence, psychosomatic ailments, outright psychosis, typical of the urban hive and the Mom-Dad nuclear family. The extended family of the native village is always saner and more peaceful.

Industrial Civilization, based upon erotic inhibition and sexual domestication, is psychopathically dangerous, inevitably leading to the repression of women (it is always Eve who is to blame) and neurotic displacements of sexual charge into violent, coercive, often genocidal policies. Ashley Montague, the anthropologist, has commented ironically on the paradox: "all the civilized nations at war, all the savages at peace." It is no paradox. Repressed sex is the most violently explosive neurological blockage possible.

Contraception and conscious procreative choice give us, for the first time in history, individual decision and individual responsibility for sexual behavior. At the same time, electronic communication-technology has made it possible to link humans into social molecules and ethical collectives based, not on robotic hive-morality, but on shared evolutionary goals, consciously chosen. Both are part of the mutation that is preparing us for Space Migration. The H.O.M.E.s, of course, house the nuclear villages.

The first four neural circuits, with associated imprints and conditioned-reflex networks, are totally Euclidean, "square," concerned with adapting and preparing the newborn to survive in the spatially polarized and hive-dominated terrestrial environment. They will not be adequate for outer space.

Circuit I "consciousness" masters forward-back strategies for survival; the first dimensions of Euclidean space.

Circuit III "mind" masters right-left polarities of the nervous system itself. Right-hand preference and associated left-brain dominance creates Euclidean, Aristotelian, linear modes of "reality"-definition.

These stages "place" the nervous system in three spatial-psychic dimensions; the fourth stage "personality" mediates the evolution of the genetic seed in time by domesticating sexual behavior on a "moral" chess-board of squares and dogmatically marked "right" and "wrong" by the infallible authority of the Hive.

The function of the emerging larval nervous system is to focus, to select, to

Ours is not just another civilization falling; it is a Post-Terrestrial Prometheus rising.

narrow down, to choose from an infinity of possibilities those spatial tactics, those survival-security strategies, those sequences which insure life and reproduction here in this local place of birth and growth. The infant is cellularly prepared to learn any language, master any art or science, play any sex-role, but is imprinted to fixate, follow, mimic the narrow offering of hive parochiality.

In so doing, four-brained humanity has paid a heavy price. They kept the Seed alive, they kept the gene-pool growing, but they lost the endowment of free choice and change. In less poetic terms, larval imprinting and ocnditioning focus awareness-potential on a trivial fragment of the possibilities for intelligence and experience in a 110-billion-cell bio-computer capable, for instance, of vast right-lobe meta-programs for Hedonic Engineering (Circuit V), psionic-neuroelectric multi-phase-intelligence (Circuit VI), genetic-evolutionary wisdom (Circuit VII) and meta-physiological synergetic fusion with Higher intelligences (Circuit VIII).

One-half of the nervous system, unimprinted and unconditioned, is kept from consciousness by the right-hand left-lobe imprints and sex-role robotry. The awakening of this repressed half of our heads (the "Buddha-Mind" of the East, the "Silent Self" of Western occultism) does not signal a return to high barbarism and Macho Boy's-Adventure-Storyism, as was hoped by Nietzsche and Crowley, hysterically dreaded by Gilder and Decter. **It is not just another civilization falling; it is a Post-Terrestrial Prometheus rising.**

Behind the surface froth noted by the newspapers and the superficialities of hip-vs.-square, old-vs.-young, right-vs.-left, the new consciousness being born in the West as a result of turning on to Eastern brain-science will transcend terrestrial reality. It will not be Eastern-passive-**yin** (right lobe) or Western-aggressive-**yang** (left lobe), but **both**—entering Inner Space and Outer Space simultaneously, balancing the symbolic-rational mind of the third circuit with the Dionysian rapture-mind of the fifth circuit. It will be scientific in essence and science-faction in style. It will be based on the expansion of consciousness, the deliberate self-disciplined raising of intelligence, new understanding and control of the nervous system, and will produce a quantum leap in joy, courage, security, warmth, curiosity and sense of humor.

Neurogenetic awareness will accelerate and finally resolve the angers, confusions and injustices in the old racist and sexist imprints, by making our Declaration's "pursuit of happiness" a scientifically tangible, neurologically attainable goal.

The Post-Hipster Age will seek revelation and Higher Intelligence not in crude rituals addressed to anthropomorphic deities (Mommy and Daddy

All through history we have been going somewhere, as a domesticated society. Now we are going everywhere, in many different post-domesticated groups.

magnified) but in natural processes, the nervous system itself, the mysteries of sex, the genetic code, and especially in post-terrestrial exploration and communication.

And what will replace the Mom-Dad nuclear family? The question itself is larval, four-brained, an example of what McLuhan calls rear-view-mirrorism. The only question that need concern you is: what will replace it in your case? Or will you consciously, intelligently continue it? (It has well-known survival value and merits we do not deny.) All through history we have been going **somewhere**, as a domesticated group. Now we are going **everywhere**, in many different post-domesticated groups.

O'Neill's space-cities, within half a century, will exhibit a spectrum of sexual patterns duplicating everything that has ever existed on earth: group marriage, sexual communism, polygamy, polyandry, Gay Pride (longevity will solve the Gay problem of survival as a self-contained culture without genetic link to the heterosexual hive), Amazonian female communes, etc. and dozens, later hundreds and thousands, of sexual groupings never tried under grim survival conditions on primitive planet Terra.

The categorical imperative of Kant asked: what is right for **all** men and **all** women? This is the key ethical question of terrestrial domesticated humanity; but it is now obsolete. The post-terrestrial question is individualized: what is right and wrong **for me**, and how do I find the other free, growing, post-larvals who also want to combine and explore in that particular multi-dimensional timespace continuum? In simplest terms, the meek indeed shall inherit the earth, and domesticate it totally in Maoist-insectoid fashion. The bold shall migrate to H.O.M.E.s (High orbital mini earths) aloft.

PART 2

THE DAWN OF
CYBERNETIC POLITICS

Starseed:
A Comic Psy-Phy Comet Tale

October 1973
Folsom Prison

"Kohoutek will have a pale blue and yellow tail stretching out for somewhere between 75,000,000 and 100,000,000 miles—the yellow portions of it in the shape of a scimitar. It will first be seen by the naked eye in mid-November and will look dull. But since it will be approaching the Sun at 250,000,000 miles an hour, it will brighten and from mid-December to Dec. 28 the peoples of the world will have the finest Christmas star ever."

How about that, Chump? Do you still believe everything out there "just happened by accident."

— A "memo from a devout Christian to a friend who is an atheist" in Bob Considine's September 16 column in the San Francisco *Examiner & Chronicle.* The quoted paragraph is from a release by the American Museum—Hayden Planetarium

The signal is being transmitted from a cell in Folsom Prison, which is the Black Hole of American society. A Black Hole is a dense space with a heavy gravitational pull. Matter which falls into a Black Hole fades from view and disintegrates in the stress of gravity. Given sufficient time, its radiation becomes too feeble to be detected from without. Although the matter of the Black Hole cannot re-escape as matter, some of it may manage to escape in the form of feeble red radiation. Some cosmologists suggest that Black Holes

Life is an interstellar communication network. Life is disseminated through the galaxies in the form of nucleotide templates. These "seeds" land on planets, are activated by solar radiation, and evolve nervous systems.

are the link to another realization of matter. They may be passageways to another universe, just as the manholes of Paris lead to a world beneath the street. Well, the maximum security prison is a fine place from which to scan the universe. It's beyond pure, undiluted bad. As good as bad can be.

In here, beyond good and evil, one sees America in pain, injured nervous systems propelling robot-bodies in repetitious, aimless motion along paths labeled rights and wrong. I watch hardened criminals watching Ehrlichman on television protesting that his personal rights have been violated.

Sri Krishna Prem, the wisest man in India, sat on the floor of his little mountain-top ashram showing me pictures from medieval alchemical books. He pointed to the design of a man standing naked with devil on one shoulder, angel on the other. He said, "When you understand that, you can go on to the next lesson."

The next lesson was a parable about a great castle that was separated from shore by a swamp. Pilgrims, searchers, warriors seeking the castle disappeared into the marsh because each rock they stepped on sank from view. The Hero and his mate sat on the bank and watched for days. Then SHe rose and held his hand to Hir. He whispered the instructions that Sri Krishna Prem transmitted to me: "Leap from rock to rock more swiftly than they sink. The trick is simple. Have courage and keep moving."

Each spot we stand on crumbles beneath us, becoming a launching pad for the next stride.

From the far future. We transmit these messages back to planet earth. Beware of the Hindu trap. It's anti-sexual. The guru, god, and the swami universe is a soft, sweet custard mush. Undifferentiated unity. True unity is contacted through increasing precision of distinctions. Psy-phy. Philosophy of science. The universe is not chaos ruled by casual chance. The Second Law of Thermodynamics is pessimistic nineteenth century fraud. Higher order structures emerge and lawfully evolve because of the underlying magnetic charging. Positive-negative. WoMan.

Life is an interstellar communication network. Life is disseminated through the galaxies in the form of nucleotide templates. These "seeds" land on planets, are activated by solar radiation, and evolve nervous systems. The bodies which house and transport nervous systems and reproductive seeds are constructed in response to the atmospheric and gravitational characteristics of the host planet, the crumbling rock upon which we momentarily rest.

Evolution is concerned with nervous systems and the sexual attractive efficiency of bodies, the expansion of consciousness, Intelligence Increase.

The human being is the robot carrier of a large brain, conscious of being conscious. A robot designed to discover the circuitry which programs its behavior.

The human being is the robot carrier of a large brain, conscious of being conscious. A robot designed to discover the circuitry which programs its behavior. The nervous system is the instrument of consciousness. When humans discovered the function and infinite capacities of the nervous system, a mutation took place. The metamorphosis from larval earth-life to the next stage. The person who has made this discovery becomes a time-traveler. A Psy-Phy entity. When Astronaut Mitchell saw the blue jewel of earth against the black velvet expanse of interstellar distance, he became Psy-Phy. Ecology is a low-level distraction. Psi-Phy boy scouts picking up trash. The genetic goal is Brain-Intercourse. Electronic sexuality. Reception and transmission of thought waves. The erotics of resonance. The entire universe is gently, rhythmically, joyously vibrating. Cosmic Intercourse.

This is a message of hope and interstellar love from the Black Hole. Irrepressible optimism. Yes, it is true that repressive pessimists now (1973) control planetary politics. This is a larval phase. Life has been evolving for three and a half billion years and has just reached the half-way point. I hope.

This message of neurological resonance can be censored, imprisoned but cannot be crushed because it comes from within, from the DNA nucleus inside each cell. From the evolving nervous system. The Higher Intelligence has been seeded on planet earth and its script is writ within our bodies, emerging in every generation.

In 1963, we began searching for a spot on this planet where a station could be set up for time experiments. In that year, we were expelled from Harvard, from Mexico, Dominica, Antigua. No crimes alleged or committed. Just too much information transmitted. Blew out the local fuses.

In 1966, G. Gordon Liddy led several midnight raids, helicopter assaults on our center at Millbrook, New York. We were literally under siege. No evidence of illegal activity was found, but I was forced to leave the county. G. Gordon Liddy promoted to the White House on the basis of this harassment. The relentless web of Mind Mirror. Thus, Rosemary and I and Dylan helped to create Watergate. Howard Hunt was a White House narcotic's expert, directing the campaign of surveillance, raids, and arrests, which eventually drove us to exile in Algeria and Switzerland.

Too much energy. Keith Richards and Anita reported the same problem. Exiles on Main Street. The only solution seemed to be a boat. A new society of timeships, sailing the high seas. The Noah myth. Premonitory preparation for the emigration from planet earth. Load the boat with transmitting equipment. Sail around the Mediterranean and out to sea. Radio Free Earth.

I sat in the dim light of solitary confinement and wrote a complete systematic philosophy: cosmology, politic, epistemology, ethic, aesthetic, ontology, and the most hopeful eschatology ever specified. I hope.

At the Kabul airport the official from the American embassy grabbed my passport illegally and the Afghani police busted me for not having a passport. We were kept under armed guard for three days and driven to the airport. The Afghani policeman wept alligator tears and the Army Major told me the pilot of the airplane would return my passport.

Armed American police agents escorted me back to prison. Dumped in a solitary confinement cell for four months I wrote *Neurologic*. At the escape trial I testified under oath that I felt like a man from the 21st century being boiled in a pot by superstitious savages. Now is the time in the Sci-Fi books for the cosmic intelligence agency to send the extra-planetary rescue ship. Help!

The first time I visited the Folsom Prison library I picked up Lovell's book on outer space. The last chapter presents a drawing of the remnant of a living organism found on a meteorite. A nucleic acid molecule. The first signal from extra-terrestrial life. Help is on the way. Prisoners began to etch the design on silver pins and leatherwork handcrafted in the hobby shop. We called it STARSEED. The symbol of Psi-Phy.

In early July the New York **Times** carried a story about a newly discovered comet entering the solar system. Unexpected. Named after its finder, an East European astronomer, it would be visible during the fall of 1973 with a brilliance greater than the full moon. Kahoutek was the name.

Here, they said, was the greatest astronomical event in recorded history appearing right on schedule. We named it Starseed, new light, new life, bright reminder of our extra-terrestrial origin and future. Symbol of escape from prison.

As the weeks went by a curious fact emerged. There was no more publicity about Kahoutek. Nothing in the scientific magazines in the prison library. No one else had read about it. I wondered if I had dreamt it out of longing anticipation. Mysterious. Why so little publicity about the greatest light in the sky? Since returning to the United States many other mysterious things had happened. Watergate began to leak two days after my incarceration. The United States began to sink in the swamp. The dollar collapsed. Food shortages. Energy crisis. Even the King of Afghanistan took a dive. Was it possible that the American government had kidnapped me back to help out?

Prison provides a clear perspective. I sat in the dim light of solitary confinement and wrote a complete systematic philosophy: cosmology, politic, epistemology, ethic, aesthetic, ontology, and the most hopeful eschatology ever specified. I hope. I kept telling other prisoners: society can't take of itself,

There exists a repression, a taboo about facing the implications of the recent scientific findings which compel a total revision of our concepts of life and of human nature. So? Let's break the taboo!

itself, so it can't take care of us. It's up to us to provide the vision. It always happens this way. New light fron the Black Hole.

And nobody said anything about the comet.

Then Paul Kantner, our Jeffersonian Starshipper, sent me a report:

"On March 7, 1973, Dr. Lubos Kohoutek, a Czechoslovakian astronomer, at Hamburg Observatory, Bergedorf, West Germany, discovered a new comet. As with most modern discoveries, this one was made photographically. Later, a prediscovery image plus numerous subsequent ones have enabled astronomers to compute the comet's orbit with considerable precision.

"During July through September, it will be too close to the sun's direction for optical observation, but in mid-October, at a distance of about 168 million miles from the sun, its brightness should increase to a magnitude of between 8 and 12. From then on it should brighten quickly and is expected to reach naked eye visibility about mid-November. It will then be in the morning sky, in the south-east, about two hours before the sun (from San Francisco).

"It is not possible to predict with precision what form the comet's tail will take nor what brightness it will attain, but indications are that it will exceed that of Halley's comet, last seen in 1910 and not due again until 1986. There is a possibility that its magnitude at perihelion (closest to the sun—only about 13 million miles) may approach that of the full moon, making it one of the brightest ever seen by man."

This confirmed the hope but renewed the question: why the silence, the lack of interest? The newspapers were filled with stories anticipating the advent of the football season. Another sign of the times. The philosophic perspective has been lost. There exists a repression, a taboo about facing the implications of recent scientific findings which compels a total revision of our concepts of life and of human nature. Einstein's equations. Nuclear energy. The revelation of DNA code as literally a code to be deciphered. Neurological imprinting. Antimatter. Humanity clings to the old myths, avoids the new truths.

It happened before.

"Towards the end of the sixteenth century, Giordano Bruno aroused the groggy world, asking it to fling its mind far beyond the planets. He speculated that the cosmos extended to infinity.

"This in itself was not so shocking: but Bruno went considerably farther—he postulated a multiplicity of worlds: suns and planets with life, unseen companions for the race of man. He toyed with man's conception of himself: for this, and for magical claims and political entanglements, he was burned in 1600."

The Discovery of Our Galaxy, Charles Whitney.

THINK FOR YOURSELF   *ESCAPE THE GENE POOLS*

It is likely that extra-terrestrial signals will be received by the instrument which has evolved over three billion years to pick up electro-magnetic vibrations. The human brain itself.

"Shortly before Bruno's death, in 1600, Tycho Brahe made the first announcement of a 'new' star in the sky. A few years later he observed a comet, and proved that it moved among the planets, thus he shattered the crystalline spheres which had been supposed to carry the planets and stars about the heavens."

Tycho's star set off excited controversy because it forced a change in the cosmology. Current theories held that the stars were fixed. But the new evidence was there flashing in the sky. The stars moved. Cosmology is not a peripheral hobby, specialty of scientific experts. Every aspect of human life is based on the answers to the cosmological questions: where did we come from? Where are we going? Tycho's star appeared exactly where Christendom was unsettled by the Reformation. Luther's challenge to the immovability of Catholic theology. You could get busted those days as Galileo discovered, for advocating the idea that the earth moved.

We recall the irritation of the Air Force with U.F.O. reports. The negative finding of the Condon report that no extra-terrestrial sightings had been confirmed, was not surprising. What disturbed was the obvious emotional bias, the fact, and this is the crucial experimental datum, that the Air Force didn't want people thinking about extra-terrestrial intervention. Just as the Catholic hierarchy and its Scholastic philosophers four hundred years ago didn't want people thinking that the stars might move. The ancient, basic cosmological fears and hopes. If you start speculating about Higher Intelligence visiting planet earth, a galaxy of embarrassing issues get raised. What would the celestial visitors think of how we are running the planet? Whose selfish securities and biased superiorities would be threatened?

The Air Force U.F.O. study included, indeed, emphasized, a factor which infuriated the "flying saucer" partisans. A team of psychologists studied the personalities of those who reported the sightings. How clever of the Air Force to suggest that those whose cosmologies, however vague, included the possibility of extra-terrestrial intelligence, were themselves "kooks." In wider perspective, we can only endorse the Air Force psycho-diagnostic attempt. It may be that the contact with extra-planetary intelligence, the discovery of the master plan will not come via radio telescopic contact. And certainly the anticipation of "saucers" transporting humanoid bodies is naive. It is more likely that extra-planetary contact will be received by the instrument which has evolved over three and a half billion years ago to pick up electro-magnetic vibrations. The human nervous system itself. The Air Force psychiatrists might have done better if, instead of administering Rorschach personality tests, they

"The simplest thing would be for them to kill you," said J. Edgar Hoover's friend.
"No," I said, "the Soviet technique now is to say that the dissenter is crazy."

had performed intensive neurological examinations, brainwave studies on the wild-eyed "saucer-sighters." Maybe some of the kooks carry nervous systems receptive to a broader spectrum of electro-magnetic impulses?

I am standing in the main yard at Folsom Prison talking to a group of inmates about the Starseed conspiracy story. There is enthusiastic laughter about the Psi-Phy possibilities. We are being watched from five gun-towers by guards armed with high-powered rifles, who scan the yard with binoculars. They are especially worried when a group of convicts clusters in conversation.

Every prisoner has, during long lonely night hours, scanned the liberating possibilities of catastrophe. Folsom is near the San Andreas fault. What if nuclear war is declared?

Johnny James, a tough guy, clubs down hope. "The guards have instructions. In case of catastrophe the orders are to lock inmates in their cells and abandon the prison." Folsom Prison is half a mile below the Folsom Dam.

It is agreed that I should send out a message posing the Starseed questions. Could there be a secret conspiracy to censor extra-planetary contact? Thoughts of Dallas, Sirhan, Martin Luther King, My Lai, Cambodia, Liddy, Hunt, Haldeman, and Ehrlichman run through neural pathways. Many inmates are convinced that Hunt will never live to testify; that "they" are planning to have me killed if I start broadcasting any messages.

Walking back to the cell-block Chaslon says, "Do you know that the odds on your getting offed may have just jumped a hundred times?"

Michel-Gustav Hauchard, French swindler extraordinaire, my protector-sponsor in Switzerland, friend of J. Edgar Hoover, and admitted CIA contact, used to muse aloud: "The simplest thing would be for them to kill you."

"No," I said, "the Soviet technique now is to say the dissenter is crazy. Anyone who opposes the monolithic system must be crazy."

The old mechanical view of galaxies as accidental swirls of stars, gas and dust is giving way; signs of creative upheaval are everywhere. Stepping stones in the pool of time popping up and disappearing. When Black Holes find their places in cosmology (and local politics), neurologicians will have written a voodoo revision of the creation story.

Cosmologist Hyde now suggests that creation, or re-creation emerges, not uniformly throughout the universe, but in regions of high density and intense activity, such as a developing Black Hole. Contractions and expansions take place at scattered points within the universe. Astronomers used to think that the radiation which energizes the universe originated from Big Bangs. Now it seems possible to explain creation as the product of Black Holes.

In case of catastrophe the orders are to lock inmates in their cells and abandon the prison.

I wanted the comet Kohoutek to get me out of prison. It could be a reminder that this planet is just a brief crumbling stepping stone in the voyage of life across the galaxies. That the Higher Intelligence has already established itself on earth, writ its testament within our cells, decipherable by our nervous system. That it's about time to mutate. Create and transmit the new philosophy. Get out of jail. Please. I hope.

Behold a great light appears in the sky. The offer is made. The signal is flashed. Resonate with it or die eye-ground and bored. Get us prisoners out of here!

Bob Hyde, the strongest, wisest man in the prison system, who has sold a lot of used cars in his time, scanned this print-out and shook his head.

"Too general and inspirational. Thousands of years from now they'll point to your Starseed signal as an amusingly immature signal from the twentieth century. But right now people are confused. We want to be told what to do. Something to give our time and money to. Like Ralph Nader."

"Ralph Nader is a monster. A puritanical, moralistic, efficiency robot. We're offering the first true, hopeful cosmology in history. We gave them their nervous systems. More practical and useful than the wheel. We gave them a sign of rebirth in the sky and a Starseed symbol and showed them how to activate and hook-up their circuitry. We liberated them to escape."

"Not enough," said Hyde, who once sold two hundred repainted Philadelphia taxis in Holyoke, Massachusetts. "We want everything, but we want to pay for it. Your mistake was to give it free. We want to be told what to do."

"Let's try again," I said. "Let's see what happens when the comet appears."

But how could prisoners see the comet? At Folsom prisoners are ordered off the yard at 3:30 p.m. and spend the next 17 hours locked in their cells.

We stood around the yard discussing petitions and legal writs that would permit prisoners out of their cells at night to view the comet.

But the comet failed to show. As November changed to December, to the rains of January, newspapers reported that Kohoutek, far from full-moon brilliance, was invisible to the naked eye. Boo hoo Kahoutek!

One morning at five, I was awakened by a guard rattling the cell bars and ordered to the custody office where two federal marshall waited. "You've been subpoenaed to testify in Federal Court. We're taking you to the San Francisco County jail."

"What a drag," I said, "that's the most fucked jail in the state."

"Yeah, I know," said a marshall, "but at least you'll get to see the sunrise on the way."

Kahoutek turned out to be . . . an out-of-sight comet. Too bad!

Sunrise? The comet was scheduled to be seen just before dawn. Maybe this was a heaven-beckoning chance to see the comet.

So it happened that I sat handcuffed and leg-shackled in the rear of the marshall's car as it rolled along the East Bay freeway crunching down to look up at the Berkeley hills (where I had lived for 15 years) and the eastern sky.

Nothing to see. The dark night blue faded to silver dawn and sunlight flushed the sky pink—but no comet to be seen.

A week later, standing on the yard at Folsom, I was approached by Stupid Stan, burly, giant sub-leader of the Hell's Angels.

"Hey man, what's happening?"

"I'm dealing from my own hand," I replied.

"Out-a-sight," replied Stupid Stan.

"How you doing, man?" I asked.

"Out-a-sight," said Stupid Stan.

"Nice weather," I said.

"An out-a-sight day," agreed Stupid Stan. "Hey man, I just thought of something. You remember telling me about that comet that was going to be brighter than the full moon and fill up half the sky? I been looking out of my cell at night and I ain't seen nothing. What happened? Did someone forget to pay the light bill?"

"It turned out to be an out-a-sight comet," I replied.

"Well that's the way 1973 seems to be coming down," said Stupid Stan shaking his head. "Maybe next year, huh Tim?"

"Maybe next year," I said.

Conversations with Higher Intelligence

July 1976
At Large in U.S.A.

Commodore Tommie Dylan (agent for Central Intelligence assigned to mutational duty on planet earth) awoke, opened hir eyes and found hirself once again in a prison cell. This time it was Vacaville. Hir light-emitting diode flashed 8:00 a.m., Pacific Time. The year was 29 P.H. (Post-Hiroshima).

The Commodore yawned and stretched comfortably. She had been on the planet some 3.2 billion years and was enjoying hir middle age.

On the metal table next to hir bunk she saw the **Wall Street Journal,** brought silently every morning by Everett (stock fraud).

Dylan rose, picked up the ceramic cup containing coffee crystal, sugar and powdered cream, walked to the wash room and stirred in steaming hot water.

Returning to hir bunk she opened the brown paper bag and selected a warm, fresh-baked Danish roll redolent with melted butter and topped by strawberry jam. The rolls had been smuggled out of the prison bakery by Marshall (heroin sales).

From a silver, Chinese-inscribed case made in the prison hobby shop by Manolo (marijuana sales), she withdrew a cigarette—tailor-rolled to hir particular taste—one half Bugler for body, one quarter pipe-mix for bite, one quarter Kite for a dash of mint.

She inhaled the luxurious, rich smoke and felt welcome nicotine buzz in hir neural equipment. The Danish roll crumbled sweetly on hir tongue and the coffee soothed hir throat.

"Aren't you prepared to talk to U.F.O.'s when they arrive? Don't you really believe in Extraterrestrial Intelligence?"

After shaving, the Commodore patted hir face with the electric-sting and Byzantine scent of Chanel #5 smuggled into the prison by Jackie Dee, the cell-block barber (forgery) and turned to greet Tony (heroin possession), who was paid a carton a week to clean the cell.

Tony leaned on hir broom and initiated the daily metaphysical conversation-flying saucers, Jean Dixon, Chariots of the Gods, Swami Booboodananda, Kirlian photography, Uri Geller's key-bending, pyramid magic, reincarnation.

The Commodore's brain informed hir nine laryngeal muscles that it was time to talk more rigorously to Tony.

"Tony, I want to speak to you about something important. Are you ready?"

"Sure thing, Babe," replied Tony grinning.

"Okay. Dig this. Suppose you are walking out on the prison yard all by yourself and suddenly, KAZAM!, down comes a flying saucer right in front of you. Got it?"

"Yeah," murmured Tony, hir eyes wide open.

"And a silver stair case unfolds with a ruby-jeweled carpet and a platinum hand railing. And down walks a Superior Creature from the center of the galaxy, shining with light and wisdom.

"Whew! Far out!" murmured Tony.

"And this beautiful voice says, 'Tony, we have come trillions of light years and descended down, down into the ocean of your atmosphere to where you humans are crawling around on this swamp bottom. We have come down here to help you. And to begin, we'll answer any three questions you'd like to ask us."

Tony's eyes bulged and she laughed uneasily.

"That's far out, Babe. Say, do you believe in flying saucers?"

The Commodore's eyes flashed in mock sternness. She took two steps toward Tony and spoke in a firm voice: "Tony! Pay attention! Once in a life-time! Three questions, Tony. What do you want to ask Higher Intelligence?"

Tony's gaze fell to the unswept floor. She shuffled uneasily. After a long pause she spoke reluctantly.

"Say, Babe, are you going to the movies tonite? It's a John Wayne western!".

"Tony!" exclaimed Commodore Dylan. "Don't you have any questions to ask Higher Intelligence? All this occult reading! And all these conversations about metaphysics! And you aren't even prepared to talk to U.F.O.'s when they arrive? Don't you really believe in Extraterrestrial Intelligence?"

"Sure I do."

They say they can travel throughout our galaxy instantaneously using faster-than-light methods which they are going to teach to our quantum physicists. What's your second question?

"But you don't have your questions ready?"

Tony grinned sheepishly.

"Tell you what we'll do," continued the implacable Commodore. "You think about it and tonight you write down three questions. You bring them to me tomorrow and I'll see if I can get you the answers."

The next morning Tony failed to show up to clean the cell until after Dylan had left for hir prison job. That afternoon when they met in the mainline corridor the challenge was repeated. The following morning Tony dutifully brought hir three questions.

"Well, my first question to Higher Intelligence is, how did you get here?"

The Commodore closed hir eyes for a long minute and then spoke. "Okay, I just picked up their answer on my neural transceiver. They say they can travel throughout our galaxy instantaneously using faster-than-light methods which they are going to teach to our quantum physicists. What's your second question?"

"Well, next I want to know if they have atom bombs that they are going to drop on us."

The Commodore closed hir eyes again and then spoke. "They say that they can use nuclear energies and many other, more powerful sources which they will teach us, but that they will use these forces only to heal and help. There is nothing to fear."

"Gee, that's great," said Tony in obvious relief. "My next question has to do with Christ. Ask them if Jesus is going to return to save us."

The Commodore closed his eyes again and then spoke. "They say that nothing much can happen in the atmosphere swamp of a planet; that we must use our scientific knowledge to join them up there. They said to remind you, Tony, that Christ said that our kingdom was not of this world."

The rug in front of the radio executive's apartment door was inscribed with Jewish letters and a mezuzah was fixed to the door frame.

Rosenbaum was young, plump and very pleased with hirself. The Commodore declined lunch and drank apple juice while Rosenbaum gorged hirself on pickled fish, fried squash, spicy potato salad and rye bread. With a sigh of satiation the radio executive patted hir mouth with a napkin and smiled in princess invitation.

"So you have a script for a radio show. So tell me."

"My proposal," said Commodore Dylan, "is frankly modeled after the one event in the long history of radio-television that totally grabbed its audience,

> **"I mean that we'll dramatically announce on network radio that we've contacted Higher Intelligence from Outer Space and we'll invite listener questions and then we'll answer them on the basis of scientific fact."**

shook people up and changed their behavior. Do you know which epochal broadcast I'm thinking about?"

"Of course," said Rosenbaum with a patronizing smile. "Orson Welles' **War of the Worlds.**"

"Precisely. I've asked hundreds of people to name the most powerful media signal ever sent out and everyone comes up with that same answer. The Mars invasion. And that's my ambition. To do another Orson Welles, but better."

"Better?" said Rosenbaum, frowning. "I doubt very much if it can be done at all. Government regulations and FCC supervision. I don't see that it's possible."

"It can be done, if it avoids the two drawbacks of the Orson Welles script. First of all, the original was a negative trip. The extraterrestrials were hostile and powerfully dangerous. That caused that panic that the FCC worries about. And second, it was make believe. The script was based on a science fiction tale by H.G. Wells. What I have in mind is a program which convincingly contacts an Extraterrestrial Intelligence which is helpful, loving, and which generates uncontrollable joy and inspiration in the listeners. How can the government object to that?"

Rosenbaum frowned and lit a filter-tipped Kool cigarette. "Uncontrollable joy?" she murmured dubiously.

"And the second improvement we'd make in the Orson Welles script is this: the event would be science faction."

Rosenbaum puffed fiercely on hir cigarette and coughed challengingly. "Science faction? What's that?"

"I mean that we'll dramatically announce on network radio taht we've contacted Higher Intelligence from Outer Space and we'll invite listener questions and then we'll answer them on the basis of scientific fact."

"But that's a fraud," sputtered Rosenbaum. "You haven't really contacted Higher Intelligence."

"Ah," replied the Commodore, "who can be sure? Even those of us who are transmitting the signals won't know. The facts which science can now produce about the basic philosophic questions are far beyond and above what is routinely transmitted by the media—as far beyond Walter Cronkite as he is beyond the cave man. Science faction is stranger than fiction."

"No, it won't go," said Rosenbaum shaking hir head. "Facts are boring and don't sell. To give you the hard, marketing truth, facts are not believable or commercially marketable these days. There's no interest there."

"But how can I double my intelligence?" protested Rosenbaum. "Perhaps that should have been your first question," replied Dylan, continuing to smile.

"Well, let me try it out on you. Are you ready? Zap!" exclaimed Dylan, clapping her hands in front of the astonished radio executive's face. "Here is Higher Intelligence on the line! What three questions do you have?"

The forces of one-G gravity tugged on Rosenbaum's sagging facial muscles and hir red tongue extended, lizard-like over hir juicy lower lip. Then she smiled slyly.

"Well, first I want to know the time of my death."

Dylan responded without hesitation: "The answer to that question is simple—Higher Intelligence says that you need not die! That terrestrial science already knows enough to prolong your life-time indefinitely."

"Why that's horrible," replied Rosenbaum angrily. "The purpose of life is to die."

"The answers from above are not guaranteed to please. What's your second question?"

Rosenbaum smiled broadly. "My second question is easy. When will I make a million dollars?"

"And the answer is easy," assured the Commodore. "You'll make a million dollars within a year if you syndicate these Conversations with Higher Intelligence. What's your final question?"

"Hmmm. Let me think," said the radio executive, fumbling with the green and white cigarette package. "How can I cope with the emotional problems of life?"

"Higher Intelligence says that you can only cope with your emotional problems by becoming twice as intelligent," said the Commodore with a smile.

"But how can I double my intelligence?" protested Rosenbaum.

"Perhaps that should have been your first question," replied Dylan, continuing to smile. "I must say, your Questions were quite materialistic. You know, sometimes people ask scientific questions, like the formula for exceeding the speed of light and so forth."

"Well, I'm a very materialistic person," said the radio executive.

Gabriel Wisdom, disc jockey for KGB-San Diego, skillfully parked his Datsun station wagon on a cliff above the beach.

"We can walk from here. Shall we take surf boards?"

"No. We'll body surf the brain waves today," replied the Commodore as she stepped out of the car.

They were both dressed in swimming garb and both were tanned darkly. Wisdom's hair, beard and body fuzz bleached to blonde and Dylan's silver and

---

"How are we going to get the voice of Higher Intelligence on tape?"

and black. They walked along the sidewalk, hot against the soles of their feet, and then climbed down the steep cliff. The secluded beach was deserted except for groups of surfers, Southern California men with long blonde hair and bodies polished and smoothed by the incessant massage of sand and sea. And women with long, smooth cocoa limbs who casually floated by to chat affectionately with the disc jockey and the Agent from Central Intelligence, both of whom were legendary figures to the graceful shoreline creatures.

"Surfers understand the nature of energy better than any other group," said Gabriel Wisdom walking along the shore. "No guru or swami, no other yoga is so pure and precise. And they all love you."

"That's because I'm a surfer too. Riding the waves of evolution. It's the simplest job to be a cybernetic brain surfer. Just open your eyes and see how the next genetic wave is coming in."

"And ride it in," said Wisdom, laughing.

"Without getting trapped or confused by the ebb-tide between waves."

"Like the Nixon reaction?" said Wisdom. "When is the next wave coming?"

"Soon," said the Commodore. Can't you feel it gathering? And it's going to be a big one. It will make the 60s look like a ripple."

The two cuties had walked the length of the beach and stood at the edge of a wide platform of black stone stained with bright green moss. They watched sea rush into narrow crevice, surge up through blowhole with high, feathery spumes of white covering bodies of children and surfers sitting against the cliff, shouting and laughing with wet shock.

The disc jockey and the Commodore sat on the sand with their backs against the cliff.

"I have only one technical question," said Gabriel Wisdom. "I can do the newscaster who interrupts the regular program to announce that Higher Intelligence is sending radio messages to a 13-year-old kid in Los Alamos. And we'll tape the kid's voice by phone. And you'll play the on-the-spot correspondent. But how are we going to get the voice of Higher Intelligence on tape?"

"I've always assumed that the Voice of Higher Intelligence would be female."

Gabriel Wisdom laughed with pleasure. "Or how about the voice of a child?"

Both cuties laughed. The Commodore was stroking the warm sand with hir hand.

"And another question . . . I mean . . . how is it going to sound . . . I mean it's gotta sound real . . . how is it going to be real?"

'She's good,' thought Dylan. 'She's an actor. And she plays with hir throat like a stringed instrument. No, more than that, like a sexual organ.'

"You know," said the Commodore, "I love this here. The sea, the sand, and the hot caress of the sun on my skin. This is the way to work. Don't you feel the same way?"

"I guess I take it for granted," replied Wisdom.

"But it's going to be real," said Dylan. "The human brain is a transceiver. It's basic function is to pick up and transmit signals from Higher Intelligence. If we can just set up the right conditions and get a brain open to transceive."

The Commodore stood just before midnight in the center of the broadcasting studio of KGB. Behind hir, the News Room was dark. To hir right, through the window, she could see Gabriel Wisdom seated in front of console panels twisting dials, selecting records, speaking in a low mellow voice to the AM audience. To her left through the glass she could see Micky Sheehy in the FM booth spinning rock and roll.

At midnight both announcers emerged from their booths, Gabriel disappearing in a production room to tape the late news. Micky Sheehy, retiring to another production room to tape a shoe-store commercial, waved Dylan to follow.

The Commodore watched from the door as Sheehy, earphones over hir head, sat in front of the console, mouth ten inches away from the obscenely bulbous, foam-padded microphone. Sheehy cleared hir throat, rocking gently back and forth, crooning into the mike she psyched hirself in a trance-like voice pouring out sonorous, majestic poetry about the Everlast Shoe Line.

She's good, thought Dylan. She's an actor. And she plays with hir throat like a stringed instrument. No, more than that, like a sexual organ. When the red, NOW-RECORDING light blinked out Wisdom opened the door and motioned to the Commodore.

The two cuties walked to the new production room, where the fifteen-year old girl was waiting.

"Have you read over your script?" asked Gabriel.

The girl nodded tensely.

She's nervous, thought Dylan. That's good. She has every reason to be.

The girl sat in front of the console. Gabriel fiddled with the dials and punched the tape buttons making loud clicking sounds. She nodded ready. Dylan read the cue lines and the girl addressed hir welcome to Higher Intelligence.

When the girl was finished Dylan took hir place and read hir lines interviewing the girl.

Gabriel punched the rewind button and the tape spun back with a whining screech. The two cuties and the girl listened to the interview.

"Remember," said the Commodore, "you're a billion miles away and you're right here in our window pane. You're an ancient creature of the galaxy."

Wisdom hit the rewind button and nodded. "That stuff is good. I can edit it smoothly, dub in the background excitement noises, murmur of voices and so forth. And I can do the breathless newscaster. But we still need the voice of Higher Intelligence."

At that moment the door to the studio opened and Sheehy walked in.

She's your basic, successful hip talent, thought the Commodore. **Superskeptical. Totally cynical about hype. A fine audio craftsman. But jaded. Turned on, but no where to tune it in. And she's Irish. That's a break. The Celts are the only ones who really believe in heaven and immortality.**

"Tell me, Sheehy. How would you like to be the voice of Higher Intelligence from Outer Space?"

Sheehy nodded with a grin and moved to the chair in front of the mike.

"Why not? Let's give it a try."

Commodore Dylan handed the script to the disc jockey. Sheehy began reading. Leafing through the pages she smiled, nodded, then broke out into a laugh.

"This is heavy stuff," she said. "You know, we could add an echo, just a tiny bit to give it texture and phase over it to give a hollow, wavering, interstellar effect."

Gabriel Wisdom nodded and strung a fresh tape through the recording machine. Sheehy cleared hir voice and leaned towards the mike. Dylan and the girl stood in front of hir watching intently.

Sheehy began to read the script softly, adjusting sound levels. She closed hir eyes and repeated the lines. Then she looked up.

"Would you mind moving back out of my line of vision? I want to get myself into this part."

"Remember," said the Commodore, "you're a billion miles away and you're right here in our window pane. You're an ancient creature of the galaxy. You're the great Mother-Father in the sky talking down to this infant race. Teaching these children whom you love and cherish."

Sheehy nodded and started putting herself into trance, reading and re-reading the first lines, slowly increasing the volume, juicing up the vibrato, the sonority. Your omniscient, genial, all-wise sexy radio voice laying it down. Suddenly she broke off.

"Look, I'm having some trouble reading the pencil additions. Could we have the script typed on the big machine in the news room?

Dylan nodded and took the script into the news-room. She sat in front of the manual typewriter and slowly, precisely tapped out the first speech from the Higher Intelligence in giant script of the cue-print machine. She ripped the first

Sheehy stood transfixed, hir mouth half open in amazement. "You know," she said slowly, "I'm a believer. That sounds real to me."

speech out of the machine and rushed to the studio. Sheehy took it without a word and turned to the mike, vanishing into auto-hypnotic trance.

Dylan returned to the newsroom to type the next speech.

For the next half hour the routine continued, Sheehy taking each speech, losing herself in some neural tract between brain and vocal cords.

When the last transmission was finished Sheehy pushed back from the mike, took a deep breath, and turned to the tape, flicking the rewind button. "This thing is getting me more and more involved," she said to Wisdom. "Let me dub in the phasing."

Headphones circling hir face, hands twisting the dials, Sheehy sat listening with a faint smile on hir face.

"Okay. Let me rewind and we'll listen to what God has wrought." Sheehy stood, removed the headphones and walked to the recording console. The Commodore, Wisdom, and the girl waited while the rewind tape whined. When it flicked to stop, Sheehy punched 'Play' and the small room cornered by quadrophonic speakers suddenly boomed with thunderous sound-waves amplified by electromagnetic power.

HELLO PLANET EARTH. THIS MESSAGE IS BEING SENT FROM THE CENTER OF YOUR GALAXY. CONGRATULATIONS. LIFE ON SOL-3 HAS NOW EVOLVED TO THE POINT WHERE THE HUMAN RACE IS READY TO COMMUNICATE WITH YOUR NEIGHBORS, LEAVE YOUR TINY, RESTRICTING WOMB PLANET, AND JOIN THE GALACTIC COMMUNITY. THIS IS A MOMENT OF GREAT CELEBRATION FOR US WHO HAVE WATCHED YOU GROW ... AND IT IS A GREAT MOMENT FOR YOU WHO ARE ABOUT TO GRADUATE TO A HIGHER LEVEL. THE HUMAN RACE, AS AGENT FOR ALL LIFE ON YOUR PLANET, IS NOW ABLE TO LEAVE THE WOMB AND TO BE REBORN AS GALACTIC CITIZENS. WE, YOUR NEIGHBORS AND RELATIVES, SHALL BE TEACHING YOU, HELPING YOU GROW. YOU, AT STATION KGB, HAVE BEEN SELECTED TO ACT AS RADIO CONTACT, TO RECEIVE AND SEND SIGNALS BETWEEN THE HUMAN RACE AND YOUR FRIENDS OUT HERE.

Sheehy stood transfixed, her mouth half open in amazement. "You know," she said slowly, "I'm a believer. That sounds real to me."

"It figures," said the Commodore dryly. "Galactic Intelligence naturally assumes the voice of a radio announcer."

"Is this going to be aired?" asked Sheehy.

"We plan to get it syndicated," replied Gabriel Wisdom cheerfully. "We're going

Sheehy stood silent, frowning. "You know . . . some religious people might not like this. It's too . . . authentic. We could get in trouble with this."

to ask all the listeners to write in and ask three questions of Higher Intelligence."

"Why not," added Commodore Dylan. "Everyone I know is bored at the level of conversation down here. We think that a lot of people are ready to start talking to Higher Intelligence. It's like tennis. You're better off playing with someone better than yourself."

Sheehy stood silent, frowning. "You know . . . some religious people might not like this. It's too . . . authentic. We could get in trouble with this."

"Not **we**," said the Commodore, smiling. "**You** could get in trouble. I've been through that scene already and my dues for the broadcasting unions are paid in full. This time I'm just going to write the script."

Sheehy laughed. Everyone laughed.

War and Centralization
as Necessary Prelude to Space Migration

March 1976
Federal Prison San Diego

Post industrial civilization now faces in the most practical, market-place form, basic directional species questions which formerly could be relegated to irovy-tower philosophers.

Hey there, you driving down the freeway. Tell me. What is the meaning of life?

And you there, kicking back to read this chapter. What is the goal of evolution? Where are we going?

And, by the way, with what basic elements is our universe programmed? And what are the basic programming algoriths of this, our universe? Can you deal with the Edward Fredkin and William Gibson notion that the intelligence that inserted this algorith is waiting, like the rest of us, to watch it run and see how it turns out?

Before 1945 (and today in countries which have not yet mastered the quantum-thought technologies of the 20th century), four less philosophic issues have kept our species ener-genetically preoccupied:

1. Bio-Survival: How do we stay alive?

2. Territorial Control and expansion: Belfast, Ireland, Golan Heights, Afghanistan, Nicaragua, Malvinas.

3. Technological Competition: Japanese computers, German cars, Swiss watches.

4. Cultural Homogenization: 150 million Americans watching **Rambo**, 150 million Russians reading **Pravda's** denunciations of **Rambo**.

All over the planet various gene-pools are moving through stages, often painfully. In 1988, for example, China seems to be moving from a Feudal to Industrial state, while the USSR creakily tries to move into the post-industrial stage.

1. Bio-Survival Has Been Solved By Almost All Gene Pools

Bio-survival is the first goal of every species. When faced with starvation or threatened by violence neither the wild wolf nor the domesticated human wonders about evolution and the meaning of it all. The issue is to stay alive. Now, however, medicine, public health and mechanical agriculture have dramatically increased life expectancy. **Global war has been eliminated** as a species threat. In its boredom and crowded abundance, post-technological

In "Gravity's Rainbow" Thomas Pynchon brilliantly demonstrates how neuro-technology became the motivating force behind the seemingly irrational convulsions of the 20th century.

society has had to exaggerate and dramatize bio-survival fears which are transmitted by the entertainment industry to titillate the protected. Crime shows. Detective novels. Horror movies. Scary roller coasters. Jaws. Car racing. Conspiracy theories. AIDS panics. Glamorized highjackings and USA terrorist raids on Grenada, Libya, Bolivia, Nicaragua. Ecological doomsdaying, government sponsored terrorism.

Now that science has almost eliminated the causes of bio-survival insecurity, the navigational question returns: "You there reclining in comfort reading this essay: answer me, survival for what?"

2. Territorial Expansion and Control Are No Longer Goals of the Post-Industrial Human.

During the last 2000 years the population of our species has increased in number and expanded in geographical spread. Up until 1946, politics—i.e. neuromuscular mastery of territory and other humans (slavery in its many forms)—preoccupied human consciousness.

The great political conflicts—war, conquest and enslavement—were, some say, necessary stages of neural evolution. Xenophobia (i.e. territorial jealousy) may be a natural phase through which mammalian species must pass.

Political ideology—nationalism, imperialism, class struggle, partisan conflict, gene-pool chauvinism—as a goal of life is now out-dated. Police and military control assure that there will be no more big conquests or dramatic revolutions involving industrialized countries. Surely it is obvious that almost every civilized country now has the land and the government its people deserve. The Chinese like insectoid Maoism. The Russian people apparently adore authoritarian centralization. We Americans apparently prefer the televised popularity contest.

(This is not to say that civilized people are happy. Far from it. The more socialized the country, the more morose and bored the quality of life.)

3. Technological Competition becomes Global Conglomerates

During the 20th century politics was replaced by technological rivalry as the goal of life.

In Gravity's Rainbow Thomas Pynchon brilliantly demonstrates how neuro-technology became the motivating force behind the seemingly irrational convulsions of the 20th century.

The politics and suicidal tactics of World War I seem inexplicable, indeed, almost comic-opera, until one realizes that the real issues were neurogenetic-technological. The national competitions of 1914 compelled the antagonist

> ... **the stages of emerging technology on this planet, including technological warfare, are standard and inevitable stages in the development of nervous systems on nursery planets like our own.**

countries to master the tank, the airplane, radio and the rapid transportation of masses of people.

The political line-ups of World War II seem equally absurd until we understand that the genetic purpose of the conflict was to stimulate the development of radar, rocketry, synthetic chemistry, atomic fission, long-range naval maneuvers and accelerated aeronautics, and, most important, computers and digital linguistics.

As soon as World War II ended, like magnetized iron-filings, the victorious centralized states immediately and magically lined up in new polarized competitive order. Actually, the Cold War increasingly lost **political** meaning as America catapulted towards centralized welfare socialism and Russia moved towards a consumer middle class. The rivalry from 1945 to 1975 involved nuclear fusion, computer flight control, intercontinental missilery, bio-chemical-genetic research, sophisticated electronics and space flight.

We see, now, that centralized governments require diligent, competent, mechanically efficient middle-classes to mobilize the technology necessary for Space Migration, Intelligence Increase and Life Extension (S.M.I.²L.E.).

Without totally endorsing Samuel Clemens' technological mysticism ("we grow back-bones when it comes back-bone time"), let us consider the possibility that every aspect of neuro-technical evolution has been pre-programmed by DNA, that the stages of emerging technology on this planet, including technological warfare, are standard and inevitable stages in the development of nervous systems on nursery planets like our own.

4. Cultural Homogeneity Is A Dead End

The structures of the evolving human body-brain and the outcomes of its changing interaction with the chemical-physical resources of a routine planet like Sol-3 are, I suspect, galactic constants. It is inevitable that technological societies, even the most communist-Spartan, produce a technical-consumer culture. People who work during the day in computerized factories manufacturing Soviet electronics cannot be expected to return each night to pre-industrial living quarters. Thus does technology create the electroid-homogenized society, almost insectile in its centralization. Urban Russians insist on access to electronically amplified rock and roll and [bootleg] pocket computers.

A centralized consumer civilization is an inevitable evolutionary development. But what is to come? The Russian-Chinese-European-American-Japanese citizen is approaching the point where the next post-industrial questions emerge:

Growth restriction, back-to-earth ecology and zero-population plans are clearly unsatisfactory answers, selfish, defeatist and pessimistic.

Bio-survival for what?

National security, for what?

Technological efficiency, for what?

Consumer-cultural television homogeneity, so what?

The four basic terrestrial stages seem to have been mastered. It is clear that the challenges which our species now faces are of a new order—over-population, energy shortage, nuclear proliferation, scarcity of resource, a general clogging of the social machinery, aimlessness, boredom, escapism, Rambo terrorism and T.V. passivity.

What gets lost in the pessimism is the fact that our species is riding an enormous evolutionary brain-wave, a gigantic upsurge in information-release which must be designed with some goal in mind. All the graphs reveal a sudden explosion of electronic thought-processing in the last hundred years. At the same time that most other forms of mammalian life (except the domesticated) is in danger of extinction, the human-energy chart takes off in a breath-taking launch.

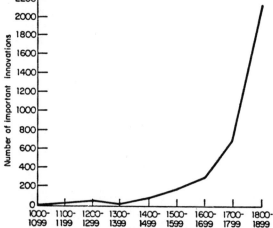

INTELLIGENCE INCREASE: The wave we are riding!

The number of important inventions and discoveries, by century from A.D. 1000 to A.D. 1900 (from Lenski, 1970, reprinted from Sociobiology by E. Wilson). Similar, but even more dramatic diagrams chart the explosive emergence of other indices of neurogenetic intelligence: altitude and velocity attained; population growth; communications networks including literacy rates; number of scientists; life-span; specialization of performance; number of electronic appliances; etc., etc.

Our species is riding an enormous evolutionary brain-wave, a gigantic upsurge in information-release which must be designed with some goal in mind.

The Next Goals of Human Life are: S.M.I.²L.E.

Exactly at the time when the four stages of terrestrial survival seem to have been mastered, centralized civilization has produced three technologies which suggest the next evolutionary goals for our species.

Space Migration relieves population pressure, uplevels territorial conflict, offers humanity unlimited energy and space—not on uninhabitable planets, but in O'Neill's space colonies.

Intelligence Increase: Modern neurology, humanistic psychology and psychopharmacology has, in the last decade, demonstrated that the body-brain is a complex bio-chemical instrument which can be understood and used to define new dimensions of consciousness and intelligence.

Knowledge of how the brain creates realities (via imprinting) makes possible self-directed brain-change and reality expansion. Quantum physics (Feyenman) merges with computer science (Fredkin's "universe as computer") and with digital psychology (Leary's *Mind Mirror, Head Coach* & Performance Books). The brain is programmed by new paradigms—the brain as reflector of the universe.

Life Extension: Micro-biology and genetics are deciphering the DNA code thus providing the possibility of rejuvenation and indefinite Life Extension. Bio-chemists assure us that there is no scientific reason why a healthy person cannot extend her-or-his life span several hundred years. Thus, in addition to unlimited **Space** and expanded **Brain** our species now faces the challenge of unlimited **Time.**

Let us briefly consider the three elements of the S.M.I.²L.E. formula that now compel us to reshape our species philosophy.

Space Migration is the Inevitable Next Step in Evolution.

The inevitability of Space Migration can be seen clearly when we compute the trajectories of species evolution, of theology, of scientific progress, and social organization. All of these systems seem to point us upwards away from the heavy pull of gravity.

The trend of biological evolution on this planet has been from water, to shoreline, to land, to atmospheric flight. Now, humanity has reached the velocity necessary to escape the G-1 pull. The nervous system has similarly evolved in contelligence. Communication has moved from close-range contact (touch-taste-smell) through distance vision to the present point where light-speed signals are routinely transceived.

Most of the religious revelations and cosmologies which have guided humanity in the past have agreed that the goals of life are to be found in "heaven above." Surely it is no accident that winged angels, celestial realms, messianic

All of the sciences provide converging data which point to the certainty that Migration from the earth is the next step in evolution.

---

descents and ascensions, are basic themes found in almost all theologies. The Higher Intelligence and humanity's destiny has always been located in the sky. Even such an occult, kabbalistic scheme as the Tarot has been so designed that the first 12 cards portray mundane personages (Emperor, Chariot, Pope) whereas the last ten cards present extra-terrestrial entities.

Science, too, systematically leads human contelligence to the recognition that humans need not be restricted to the heavy-gravity atmosphere of earth, and, indeed, that the surface of a planet is the worst place to operate a technological civilization. All of the sciences provide converging data which point to the certainty that Migration from earth is the next step in evolution.

Astronomers tell us that there are probably hundreds of millions of planets like ours in our solar system. Life forms on many of these planets, may be ahead of us in the evolutionary process, have presumably migrated from their womb planets and await us to join them in the communication networks of extraplanetary info-space.

N.A.S.A. committees have confirmed Gerard O'Neill's conclusions that the surface of a planet like ours is emphatically not the place for an accelerating industrial civilization. There are neither the resources nor the energy available down here at the bottom of a four thousand mile gravity swamp to meet the technological and material aspirations of our fellow humans. Off the planet surface, on the moon and in the asteroid belt, there awaits unlimited material resources, inexhaustible solar energy and boundless space in which to construct custom-tailored worlds.

In addition to the evolutionary, the religious and the scientific evidence is the psycho-social impulse to migrate which is manifested in almost every aspect of current pop-culture. It is as though our species senses intuitively that the great mutational movement is about to occur. The fact that two-thirds of the American polled-public believes in the reality of "flying saucers" (in spite of the unconvincing evidence of their existence) does suggest that some sort of a mutational premonition has infiltrated the consciousness of our species.

The sudden popularity of science-fiction books, space movies (Star Wars, Encounter of the Third Kind) and the inexplicable, unquittable grasp of the silly STARTREK series are media phenomena pointing to our aspirations upward. Then too, the hippy-drug-culture movement can be seen as a premature quiver of extraterrestrial consciousness. The sudden mass impulse to "get high," to float, to space-out, to trip, to avoid the "downer" seems to express the new revelation that gravity is the ultimate drag, that the "Fall" in Genesis is literally a

---

Off the planet surface, on the moon and in the asteroid belt, there awaits unlimited material resources, inexhaustible solar energy and boundless space in which to construct custom-tailored worlds.

fall, that the ultimate energization and discovery of human potential is the process of becoming a "star."

Here, as always, we meet the recurrent paradoxical nature of evolution: in order to attain the ultimate human freedom of space existence, in order to attain the velocity to escape the planet it was necessary to link up in centralized-collectives. This is the Centralization Paradox—the phenomenon which has so confused planetary politics for the last few decades. Capitalistic countries insisting that we must **organize** to counter Communism. Republican Big-business competing with Democratic Big-Government for control of the centralized economy. It is true that technology has created assembly-line societies—insectoid in its harnessing of the individual to the collective goal. But trust in the genetic design (always paradoxical when seen in the short view) may comfort us that centralization and only centralization can organize private enterprise and public structure to produce the enormously complex technology necessary to migrate from the planet. Despite the campaign rhetoric, the bureaucracies—big business and big government—are here to stay until they have served their genetic mission. The centralization effect cannot be checked. But it can be rationally directed towards our species goal: Space Migration: which in turn offers the only way to re-attain individual freedom of space-time and the small group social structures which obviously best suit our nervous systems. It is another paradox of neuro-genetics that only in space habitats can humanity return to the village life and pastoral style for which we all long.*

Intelligence Increase Is Required for Space Migration and Life Extension

Intelligence, we define, as the range and acceleration of information-bits (energy signals) received, integrated and transmitted by the MOS [the Mind Operating System]. The more intelligent the species or the individual the wider the scope and the faster and more precise the information transceived. Humans are more intelligent than other mammals because we have learned to (1) receive, (2) remember-retrieve-organize and (3) transmit by means of symbols and artifacts an enormous range of energies—microscopic, telescopic, mechanical, electro-magnetic, quantum.

The Law of Least Effort suggests that no individual or no species is any more intelligent than necessary. During certain phases of evolution and of history

---

* In the O'Neill-N.A.S.A. designs, agriculture and industry are separated from the living habitats thus returning the space colonists to small pastoral or village environments where face-to-face interactions will allow the formation of the multi-person social molecules which apparently are necessary for the synergistic linkage of humans.

Until the present time it has been downright dangerous to be too smart or let it be sensed by the collective mind that one was too effectively innovative.

(social and personal) there are periods of calculated stupidity; a coasting along on energies already mastered. Periods of repetition and stability and lazy affluence. The 1950s and the 1980s are recent periods of collective stupidity. There are other periods in the life of a species, a race, an individual when the evolutionary process forces a confrontation with the future, a challenge which demands an upsurge of intelligence, an opening-up to reception of new frequencies, new organizing principles, new methods of transmission. World War II with its sudden explosion of technological and political innovation was such a period. The 1960s with its sudden explosion of new consciousness and new cultural philosophies was another such period.

Here it should be pointed out that the DNA code guides and guards the evolutionary process using hive-instincts of conservation. The individual or the group that becomes too smart, too far advanced, is inevitably checked up to the point when the next mutation is about to happen. Until the present time it has been downright dangerous to be too smart or to let it be sensed by the collective mind that one was too effectively innovative. Eccentric geniuses are tolerated only if isolated in ivory-towers and if they make no attempt to rock the species boat or to corrupt the young with new ideas.

At times of species mutation and genetic challenge there is a sudden eruption of innovation. The 6th century B.C. produced Pythagoras, Buddha, Lao-Tse. The Elizabethan and Renaissance period in Europe and the Islamic eruption of the 9th century A.D. were similar explosions of mutation and migration.

It will be noted that most periods of intellectual breakthrough and neurological mutation have occurred during epochs of migration and exploration. The DNA code, girding itself to hurl its seed outward, activates new neural circuits and allows the conservative gene-pool selfishness to relax its inertial control.

We may now be witnessing such a neurological mutation. If humanity is to migrate in space and to extend the life span we must get smarter, fast.

It is no accident that just at this point in history neurology, psycho-pharmacology, humanistic psychologies, digital physics, computer literacy, digital psychology are offering the human being the opportunity for increased understanding, liberation and control of his own destiny.

For the first time in human history, control of one's own body and of one's own life style and identity (luxuries formerly reserved to the aristocracy) is now, however thoughtlessly and trivially, an accepted right of the middle-class American.

Many of our most perceptive social critics have worried about this consumer

Has evolution labored for three and a half billion years to produce a new race of sun-tanned, organically fed, gracefully exercised, poly-orgasmic, self-actualized, somatic technicians?

efflorescence and the obvious question: what is the meaning and goal of this new philosophy of self-discovery and personal growth? Has evolution labored for three and a half billion years to produce a new race of sun-tanned, organically fed, gracefully exercised, poly-orgasmic, self-actualized, somatic technicians?

The answer, of course, is no! The Digital Intelligence which designed the DNA code does not make mistakes. When a species arrives at a comfortably secure level of success that it creates a restless, bored hedonic caste, then the next mutational pattern kicks in. [See Edward Fredkin's theories of the universe as computer and the brain as reflection of the universe.]

Somatic consumerism leads logically to brain consumerism, gourmet reality-options. Those individuals who have learned to pilot their bodies as vehicles for self-improvement and self-promotion, inevitably sense that the next stage of planful, aesthetic self-definition involves piloting the brain through the newly discovered info-worlds and digital spaces.

If there is any goal beyond narcissism for the new generation of hedonic consumers freed from the constrictions of the work-aesthetic and the old-time religions, if there is any social or genetic purpose to this new, self-conscious individualism perhaps it is in preparation for the greatest challenge our species has faced in millennia—the expansion of space and time.

Life Extension Is Only Conceivable in the Context of Space Migration and Intelligence Increase

All of the religious and philosophic systems constructed by human beings have concerned themselves with the basic issue of death. The western religions have offered immortality in a post-mortem, heavenly realm to be attained by the socially virtuous. The oriental religions, addressing themselves soberly to the gloomy fact that human life ends inevitably in sickness, senility and death, have offered passive resignation and a detached individual yoga.

Recent developments in biology and genetics have added a startlingly new perspective on this ancient preoccupation. Scientists now inform us that the human life span can be extended indefinitely and that within a few decades virtual immortality is technically possible. The first in-depth study of the implications of extended life-span appeared in a book, **The Immortalist** by Alan Harrington. The cover of this book contains a striking endorsement by Gore Vidal (never one to waste praise on fellow authors) who was led to wonder if "this may be the most important book ever written." Harrington's thesis is simple. Death is the only enemy of humanity. The conquest of death should be the basic and central concern of science. Death should be snuffed.

The conquest of death should be the basic and central concern of science. Death should be snuffed.

Life Extension, however, without Space Migration and Intelligence Increase is clearly an impossible nightmare. Until now it was necessary for post-menopausal humans to die and get their bodies off the scene to make room for the new arrivals. Is it nucleic-acid mysticism to suggest that current break-throughs in life-extension sciences are inevitably synchronous with the emergence of space technology? Surely life extension would be unthinkable without a space frontier. And with limitless space available immortality becomes a migratory tool.

No rejuvenation without migration! could well be the motto to protect us from the horrid possibility of John Denver and Frank Sinatra at age 500 still re-appearing at Las Vegas. And Richard Nixon running for the presidency for the fiftieth time, and, out of our boredom, winning!

Longevity is equally forboding without Intelligence Increase. A recent opinion poll about attitudes toward life extension revealed the surprising result that most people can't bear the idea of living longer. "My marriage can limp through another ten years," was one reaction, "but a hundred more years would be a disaster." Extended life span will obviously require a sudden quantum jump in neural efficiency, the knowledge of how to re-imprint realities, to create new identities, to absorb new mental styles, to learn new tricks.

The Parable of the Five Caterpillars and the Butterfly

These three evolutionary developments—Space Migration, Intelligence Increase and Life Extension—offer our species a chance to resuscitate our more enduring visions of challenge and grandeur; a chance to, once again, think noble, hopeful thoughts about our future

It is for this cause that we consider the parable of the five caterpillars, just before their own metamorphosis, who see their first butterfly.

The conservative caterpillar sniffs and says, "That's illegal and immoral. They should arrest that irresponsible individual and cage her down here on the ground where she belongs." ·

The technical caterpillar snorts, "They'll never get me up in one of those."

The liberal-progressive caterpillar shouts rhetorically, "How dare that frivolous creature float free when there are caterpillars in Bangladesh who don't have color T.V.'s."

The Hindu-Buddhist caterpillar chants "Ohm" in a superior manner and says, "Why go to the bother to build those wings when I can just sit in the lotus position and fly by means of astral travel."

The technical caterpillar snorts, "They'll never get me up in one of those."

And the religious caterpillar murmurs piously, "If God had intended caterpillars to fly he would have given us wings."

In Defense of "Snake Oil Salesmen"

June 1976
Pecos, New Mexico

"**We** (sic) expect to have **our** (sic) orbiting space station
planned to house two hundred **workers** (sic) by 1983-1984 . . .
We (sic) feel that public participation in its planning is
feasible."
> Jesco Von Puttkamer, N.A.S.A. Office of Space Flight

"Von Puttkamer predicted that in the building and operation
of this space station, which he sees as the crucial first step
toward the colonization of space,'. . . a lot of hardships **should**
(sic) be encountered and overcome. What **we** (sic) don't want
is for these hardships to generate a backlash. Supporters of
space colonization **should** (sic) show a measured judgement—
no snake oil salesmen are needed.'"
> L-5 News, April 1976

At the present time, as always, political-spiritual-aesthetic differences
alienate human groups. Most of these conflicts (for example Irish-Catholic
versus Belfast-Protestant, Arab versus Jew, Democrat versus Republican)
serve only to provide a sense of self-identity and escape from boredom to the
gene-pools involved and are irrelevant to the evolutionary process. Major
political conflicts, however—the cold-war blocs—are genetically useful in
that they stimulate the great monolithic powers into technological competition
which furthers the evolution of the human nervous system.

The best explanation of how technological competition, i.e. extension of
the neuro-muscular systems, operates as a basic cause of the last century of

... one ominous possibility—the restrictive limitation of post-terrestrial reality by bureaucrats who are unashamed advocates of "hardship," control and uniformity.

warfare can be found in Thomas Pynchon's **Gravity's Rainbow**, a book which serves well as an initiatory primer for Outer Space Migration aspirants.

The "Sprawl Trilogy" of William Gibson (*Neuromancer, Count Zero* and *Mona Lisa Overdrive*) and the cellular automaton paradigms of Edward Redkin serve as primers for migration to Info-space.

Since Hiroshima, territorial war as a necessary and healthy stimulus for intellectual advancement has been replaced by rivalry in info-space (computers) and outer-space (Starwars). Since Peenemunde it has been obvious that one intellectually and survivally interesting issue on this planet concerns humanity's transition to extra-terrestrial life. Since Gibson's "Neuromancer" the other great challenge is humanity's transition to inner-neurological life.

The familiar east-west competition continues, of course, on the surface of the planet. Indeed, we might speculate that such transcontinental rivalries exist on all nursery planets at that stage in evolution when neurological-primates start assembly line tool-making preparatory for post-planetary migration. But Apollo-Soyuz is probably an accurate forecast of Inter-National collaboration in Space Colonization.

> "There can be no doubt that in the future the crews of orbital stations will be international and space exploration will become a matter involving the whole planet."
> Academician V. Glushko quoted in **Izvestia**, August 1975

This cooperation among super-powers may seem, at first impression, to auger a utopian state of global harmony. We can have no doubt that Academician Glushko and our own Herr Von Puttkamer are eager to hook-up their respective bureaucracies. But evolutionary currents always run deeper than the political and it is most important that Apollo-Soyuz linkages not conceal the fact that Space Migration confronts our species with a most critical evolutionary choice.

We recall that, after 1492, the various European powers set out boldly to impose upon the new world their own bizarre national versions of reality. Thus were created such astonishing and monstrous cultural mutations as Spanish-America, Anglo-India and Amino-Uganda.

Let us have no illusions. Space Migration will produce the most intense ontological struggles our planet has seen since the reptilian-mammalian conflict of long-ago. Space Migration offers our unfinished species the opportunity to create new realities, new habitats, new neural perspectives, new worlds unlimited by territorial longitudes or geographical chauvinisms. We are surely

The upcoming conflict over the future of Space Migration may well become a debate over the future of human evolution.

indebted to Jesco Von Puttkamer for presenting in his "snake-oil" pronunciamento a clear example of one ominous possibility—the restrictive limitation of post-terrestrial reality by hard-headed bureaucrats openly opposed to enthusiasm, optimism, pluralism and poetic vision.

Archangel Von Puttkamer's lofty attempt to guard the gates of the new celestial realms is not the first attempt by hardheads to co-opt space. Shortly after the first lunar landing, Thomas Paine, head of N.A.S.A.'s Apollo program produced in his exultation one of the most partisan statements since the Reformation. "This," said Paine, "is a victory for the crew-cut guys who use slide-rules, read the bible and salute the flag." Let us applaud Director Paine who in one magnificent flight of chauvinist rhetoric manages to alienate all tax-payers who are female, non-engineers, non-Protestants, and prefer non-marine hair styles. Substitute the word "Marx" for "bible" and the N.A.S.A. version of whose reality should control space is in close agreement with Soviet planners.

Thus we see that the upcoming conflict over the future of Space Migration ("snake-oil salesmen need not apply") may well become a debate over the future of human evolution; a debate which is philosophic rather than political and finds its roots, not in transient national rivalries, but in an inevitable tension which has existed for the last several centuries and which can best be described as mechanical/technology versus post-mechanical humanism, engineering versus ecology, hard-ware versus software, control versus freedom and, to use the brilliant unconscious metaphor of Von Puttkamer, snake-oil versus motor-oil.

It so happens that for the last 30 years I have been preoccupied with this wretched misunderstanding between engineering and humanism. I have consistently and perilously attempted to personalize, neurologize, eroticize and subjectify engineers, and on the other hand to make more rigorous, precise, replicable and objective the language and thought habits of poets and philosophers. Interestingly enough, both engineers and humanists are hopelessly trapped in the wheels of their own abstractions and control mechanisms. We are led to wonder whether the solution to these rigidities which prevent engineer-bureaucrats from communicating smoothly with each other as well as harmoniously meshing with the humanists is a certain lack of neurological flexibility which can accurately be described as "snake-oil deprivation."

In the basic sense, however, this polarity between technology and humanism is artificial and statistically common-place—i.e. stupid. Is it not demonstrably true that in any generation among the bureaucratic brigades of engineers and

---

The Space Migrant's reply to the socialist's complaint is, of course, "let the meek inherit the earth; we have farther-out plans."

---

laboratory directors there are rarely more than twelve major scientists? And is it not possible that among the armies of literature professors, pop-novelists, faculty philosophers and foundation-supported theologians, there are, at most, twelve major philosophers? And do we not find that these twenty-four frontier thinkers are usually in close agreement as to the direction of human evolution and the basic nature of energy-matter? It is both the self-appointed liberal humanists and the civil service engineers who threaten Space Migration with their clashing doctrinaire opinions—the former peevishly suspecting that any escape from earth gravity is an elitist liberation from their compulsory egalitarian plans of limited-growth and intra-planetary bussing.

The Space Migrant's reply to the socialist's complaint is, of course, "let the meek inherit the earth; we have farther-out plans." To which the liberal's stern reproach is: "You have no right to float away from this planet with the ill-gotten gains you have wrenched from the poor." The obvious response to the liberals is, as always, to buy them off. When the administrators are shown that private-enterprise space migration, like 15th Century colonization, will return enormous energy riches, the distribution of which they will be allowed to administer, they will be intellectually offended but practically mollified.

The Glushko-Von Puttkamer engineer-axis will be more difficult to evade. The Apollo project, we recall, perfectly executed its genetic mission: to return moon-soil samples rich in exactly the raw materials necessary for the construction of space colonies. All this, we suspect, was a serendipitous and mildly disturbing side-effect to the N.A.S.A. planners whose visions for the extraterrestrial future we have already seen reflected in the military flavor of the Apollo launches, the stuffy exultations of Director Paine, the Viking probes and the Sky-labs, none of which include the shocking possibility that civilian Americans and their families might insist on getting into the pioneer-frontier action.

As G. Harry Stine demonstrates in his book, **The Third Industrial Revolution**, the industrialization of space opens enormous new perspectives: " . . . new industrial empires will be forged, new billionaire industrial moguls will emerge." Much more significant than the economic are the cultural possibilities of Space Migration. It is the remarkable anthropological genius of Gerard O'Neill to recognize that the establishment of thousands of space-cylinder habitations will create an enormous plurality of culture-styles and moral systems. Literally each group of colonists who band together to finance and design a Space Habitat will be moulding a new consensual reality. Within the limits of physical security the colonists can determine the political, cultural and aesthetic dimensions of the psyche-space they inhabit.

Space Migration Bureaucrats who start setting up criteria for who need not apply, need not apply themselves.

Comparisons with 15th Century colonization (Pilgrim fathers, etc.) or with the first two industrial revolutions are much too modest. The migration situation may be more accurately analagous to the movement from marine to amphibian life or from reptile to mammalian. Imagine, if you can, the snake-oil commercials at the time of amphibious migration:

TAKE ADVANTAGE OF THESE UNLIMITED REAL ESTATE POSSIBILITIES: SWAMPS, SHORELINES, FORESTS, PRAIRIES, CAVES, BURROUGHS!!! YOU CAN BE THE FIRST ONE ON YOUR BLOCK TO GROW SCALES, FUR, FEATHERS; TO SQUIRM, SCRAMBLE, LOCOMOTE ON MULTI-PEDAL APPENDAGES!!!

Von Puttkamer's diatribe against snake-oil salesmen is the bureaucrat's timid concern that politicians and voters might be scared off by visions and enthusiasms, based on the underlying assumption that governments and legislators are going to sponsor Space Migration. We do well to listen to the shrewd advice of Astronaut Russel Schweikert (published in **Co-Evolution Quarterly**) to keep government bureaucracies out of Space Colonization and rely on private initiative and personal investment of vision.

Was it not exactly "snake-oil" that stimulated the last Age of Exploration? Marco Polo returning with spices, pungents, perfumes, soft silks, strange herbs and medicaments? Upon what resinous substances was the wealth of the East India Company founded? Did not Ponce de Leon set off after the Elixir of Life? Did not Coronado seek the fabled Seven Cities of Gold?

If Space Migration is going to be anything more than insectoid bureaucracy or another Alaska pipe-line adventure controlled by the oil politicians, the lunar Mafia and the Inter-Planetary Teamster's Union, it is going to be "snake-oil" that softens the rigidity, soothes us through the moments of hardship and makes the venture one of cultural liberation and experimental diversity. We could do worse than re-read that wry little novel **Journey To The East** in which Herman Hesse suggests that each person who sets out on the great genetic voyage has his-or-her private and highly personal goal of discovery.

Upon reading Von Puttkamer's ominous "snake-oil salesmen need not apply" one's first reaction was to reply: "Bureaucrats who start setting up criteria for who need not apply, need not apply." But this is to fall into the old terrestrial competitive trap which need no longer limit us. Rather our invitation should read: Let everyone apply. Let us be open to everyone's vision. Let every group

**Every great breakthrough in the history of science has been opposed
and postponed by the most renowned scientists of the time.**

form its own social structure. If Academician Glushko and Director Von
Puttkamer wish to share a space habitat in which wild aspirations are banned—
by all means let them do so. But before condemning themselves to a post-
terrestrial reality in which "hardship and measured judgment" are the preferred
styles, let us suggest two experiments. Herr Von Puttkamer, you should review
the history of science and recall that every great breakthrough has been opposed
and postponed by the most renowned scientists of the time; and that all of the
respectable-senile predictions about the fission of the atom, the size of the
universe, the landing on the moon have consistently overestimated the
difficulties and underestimated the grandeurs.

And would it be indiscreet to ask what Mrs. Von Puttkamer and the von
Puttkamer children think about N.A.S.A. hardship versus all-out enthusiastic
commitment? If Snake-Oil is a smooth substance which makes the skin feel
good, produces pleasant squirming motions, and encourages optimistic aspirations,
perhaps director Von Puttkamer should obtain a supply (from government
approved laboratories, of course) and apply some to himself and his wife on
starry night. Then let us review the issue of who shall live in space, and how,
and why.

H.O.M.E.S. A Real Estate Proposal

Coauthor
George A. Koopman

February 1976
San Diego Federal Prison

The paradigm of "Space Migration" is an "unselfish meme."

An "unselfish meme" is an in-pregnating thought which, when inserted in a receptive brain, breeds, fertilizes, fuses with other healthy thoughts, evolves and becomes a powerful program in the person's consciousness. To continue the biological metaphor, "unselfish memes" are cells of information which follow the same survival patterns as "genes"—replicating themselves and evolving.

Let us switch to the cybernetic metaphor. Thoughts, concepts, are the software which program our brains. A "meme" is a powerful, popular item of software which many people share.

Another powerful form of thought-ware operates, not as in-pregnating "unselfish memes" but as "selfish memes," viral thoughts, malignant programs which do not mate with healthy concepts, but replicate themselves incessantly at the expense of the host-brain. These malignant "thunks" cause the hosts to feel weak, helpless, depressed, angry, paranoid eventually ending in suicide and/or homicide. Hundreds of millions of unfortunate human beings allow their brains (and lives) to be programmed by viral or malignant "selfish memes" such as "Allah," "Evil Empire," "chosen people," "Christ the Good Shepherd," "original sin," "wrath of the Lord."

One of my standard tactics in performing philosophy has been to allow my brain to be invaded by new ideas. Memes important to my development have included: "interpersonal diagnosis," "jazz," "inner potential," "consciousness expansion," "sexual fusion," "reprogramming the bio-computer."

During my imprisonment (1970-76) the fertile meme of space migration was inserted into my bio-computer by such people as Gerard O'Neal, Carolyn Meinel and Keith Henson. This mutational meme dominated my mental-programming for two years. In my writings and lectures I inpregnated millions of people with the irresistible paradigm that they might be "premature extra-terrestrials." And that Space Migration was less dangerous than crossing the North Atlantic in a small, scurvy-ridden boat which my courageous Celtic ancestors did in the mid-18th century.

The following essay is an example of transmitting the unselfish meme: "space migration."

> **The "Earth As Womb" theory also recommends itself because it is funny, pregnant with future possibility, delightfully impudent to pompous self-conceptions.**

THE TIME FOR HIGH ORBITAL MINI EARTHS

Life on Planet Earth is now being transformed by the three basic tactics of the evolutionary process:

MIGRATION

MUTATION

METAMORPHOSIS (REJUVENATION)

The movement away from the gravity-prison of our overpopulated-underenergized planet is rapidly becoming, not just a futurist speculation, but an inevitable mutational step.

Space migration is a practical necessity.

Just as the early amphibia were forced out of the primeval water onto the shoreline, so are we being squeezed off the womb-planet into extraterrestrial existence.

THE CURRENT MESSAGE OF THE DNA CODE IS: MIGRATE FROM THE NURSERY PLANET

Life is an Interstellar Communication-Information Transmitting Company. A Free Enterprise. Unlimited.

Life is disseminated planfully on planets throughout the Galaxy in the form of nucleotide info-codes called DNA-RNA. These "info-seeds" land on "farm-planets" like ours, are activated by solar radiation, and evolve nervous systems.

The bodies which house and transport DNA-code code-seeds are activated in response to the atmospheric and gravitational characteristics of host planets.

The nervous system is a tool for deciphering the genetic code.

The message of the DNA code turns out to be: MIGRATE! REJUVENATE!

EXPLORATION AND EXPLOITATION ARE GENETIC IMPERATIVES

We propose the "Earth As Womb" paradigm because there are no facts to disprove it; because the available facts confirm it; because it is in line with the **synchronicity** and **recapitulation** laws.

Synchronicity: What happens to the individual also occurs at the microscopic and telescopic levels.

Recapitulation: The first nine months of prenatal life repeat the cycle of evolution. The first 24 years of individual development repeat the four stages of terrestrial evolution: infant (marine), child (mammal), pre-adolescent (primate), post-adolescent (sexual domestication). Gene-pools also evolve through these stages—tribal, feudal, industrial, global-social. Every stage is larval, embryonic to the next. The cycle of molting-metamorphosis continues.

We must not cringe from the word "exploitation." We must exploit every stage of available information/energy to build the structure to reach the next evolutionary cycle.

The "Earth As Womb" theory also recommends itself because it is funny, pregnant with future possibilities, delightfully impudent to pompous self-conceptions. What more entertaining conceit than to suddenly discover that, in the most scientific practical sense, we are just about to be born as post industrial cybernetics! The current writhings and convulsive spasms of our gene-pools which now disturb the serenity of our planet can be seen as natural birth pains.

This planet can no longer hold us. We are crowding and fouling the nest.

Rational, socialistic plans to reduce population, restrict growth, think small and limit free expansion are unnatural and genocidal.

The growth-restriction plans so popular among bureaucrats in the 1970s are anti-evolutionary.

It is in the nature of every form of life to joyously, confidently expand and multiply.

The embryo cannot decide to stop growth and remain comfortable in the womb. Conserve energy? No way.

Expand without limit. $E = mc^2$.

The answer of Life to its restrictors is always the same:

EXPAND! EXPEND! EXPLORE! EXPLOIT! EXCHANGE! EX-SCAPE YOUR GENE-POOL!

THERE IS NO CHOICE: LIFE MUST LEAVE THE WOMB-PLANET TO SURVIVE AND EVOLVE

We plan to organize Space H.O.M.E.s (High Orbital Mini Earths) as a practical step to explore and activate new resources—internal and external to the nervous system.

Space H.O.M.E.s open up unexploited territories, new energy sources, and new stimulation for the brain. We must not cringe from the word "exploitation." At every stage of information/energy the laws of nature seem to require new and more complex engagements of elements to accelerate the evolutionary process. We **must** exploit every new level of energy in order to build the structures to reach the next cycle. The embryo ruthlessly exploits the supplies of the maternal body. The derogatory flavor of the word "exploit" has been added by reactionary political groups who wish to slow down the expansion of energy. Rhetoric aside, there has never been an example of a surviving-evolving species which did not **use all energies** available to it. Nothing can stop the surge towards Space Migration. In addition to the logical reasons for the voyage one must face the fact that we have no choice. The mutation from terrestrial to interstellar life must be made. If only because this planet is going to explode in a solar flare-out within a few billion years. Common sense trust in the wisdom of

The most exciting, least boring way to pass our time is to assume that we can develop an immortality pill, multiply our intelligence, leave the planet and contact Superior Intelligences.

the DNA code should convince us that Life wouldn't have gotten Herself into this planetary crisis without having figured a way out.

THE ONLY QUESTIONS WORTH ASKING

Here are the only questions worth consideration by any intelligent person:
Is physical immortality possible in our lifetime?
Does Superior Intelligence exist?
How can we attain these two goals?

If your answers are negative then nothing makes any difference to you except satisfaction of robot comfort, transitory ego-reward, gene-pool security.

If your answers are affirmative, then the most profitable, adventurous and hopeful prospects emerge.

Humanity now hungers for reassurance that the ancient, philosophic aspirations were not in vain.

And for reminder that there is a practical purpose for existence. What sounds like the most spaced-out fantasy becomes, upon reflection, the only sensible proposal.

Is it our destiny to die? Is there no Superior Intelligence beyond the gradual accumulation of scientific knowledge?

Longevity and rejuvenation are not only possible but inevitable productions of an evolved nervous system. Superior Intelligence will be contacted as soon as we leave the embryonic membrane of earth atmosphere.

Superior Intelligence is Us in the future.

No matter which of these software paradigms one aesthetically prefers, the fact remains that the best investment of our energies, the most exciting and least offensive way to pass our time is to assume, pretend, gamble that we can develop an immortality pill, multiply our intelligence, leave the planet and contact Superior Intelligences. From the history of science we learn that the only way a new energy is discovered is to look for it.

Indeed, do we not find exactly that for which we search? If Superior Intelligence does not exist it is time for us to create it. In ourselves, if necessary.

When millions of space migrants from every country assemble in H.O.M.E.s to work together in the dedicated search for Immortality and Superior Intelligence, the results, even if negative, cannot fail to be amusing, instructive and profitable.

There is simply nothing better to live for.

#

George A. Koopman, in 1976-77, was president of a cybernetic learning company which developed electronic technology to help people increase

The Star Seed Migration Company is a profit-making cooperative designed to be the most lucrative venture in human history.

---

intelligence. At this time he became, like myself, inpregnated by the concept of migrating to high orbit.

Being a sophisticated man of business-affairs George saw immediately that the space migration movement would follow the history of migration to the New World in the 16th and 17th centuries.

The magnitude of the operation meant that governments would have to be involved. But the success of the movement would depend upon individual free-enterprise, civilian management, and a pioneering, frontier, independent attitude.

In 1977 when George wrote the following business proposal he was not joking. He knew, and I knew, that he had a good shot at making this paradigm take form.

PROSPECTUS   **PROSPECTUS**

5,000 Shares
Per H.O.M.E.
HIGH ORBITAL MINI EARTH
Capital Stock
(Without Par)

THESE SHARES ARE SPECULATIVE IN THAT THEY INVOLVE A
HIGH DEGREE OF EVOLUTION

Prior to this offer there has been no public market for alternative evolutionary futures. The initial offering price has been determined by Central Intelligence in accordance with the most precise and reliable data available.

THESE SECURITIES HAVE NOT BEEN APPROVED OR DISAPPROVED
BY THE EVOLUTIONARY COMMISSION NOR HAS THE
COMMISSION PASSED UPON THE ACCURACY OR ADEQUACY
OF THIS PROSPECTUS.
ANY REPRESENTATION TO THE CONTRARY IS ENCOURAGED.

Price to Public
Underwriting (1)
Discount
Proceeds To Colony

Per Share $100,000. (1) $100,000. Total $500,000,000. (1) $500,000,000.

(1) These shares will be traded on the STARSEED EXCHANGE, which is underwriting this offering in exchange for the opportunity to MIGRATE, MUTATE and METAMORPHOSIZE. Any commissions earned in the evolutionary futures will be reinvested under the regulations of the Genetic Code.

Each mini-planet will have its own post-terrestrial goal. Some will stay in industrial orbit around the earth. Others will colonize the planets and asteroids. Others will leave the solar system.

Offered by
THE STARSEED EXCHANGE

The Interstellar Energy Communication Transportation Recreation Company
a better opportunity employer

The date of the Prospectus is NOW

No dealer, salesman or government agency has been authorized by H.O.M.E.s, the Underwriters or the DNA code to monopolize the colonization of space, and any representation to the contrary is amusing. This Prospectus constitutes an offer to participate in a new venture to increase options, get smarter and live forever, while having fun, making money, and evolving, except within any state or archipelago to any person or robot where or to whom it is unlawful to make such offer or solicitation. The delivery of this Prospectus shall under every and all circumstances create the distinct impression that the future is up for grabs.

IN CONNECTION WITH THIS OFFERING, THE DNA AND OUR EXTRATERRESTRIAL NEIGHBORS MAY INTRODUCE MUTATIONS, COMMUNICATIONS OR OTHER QUANTUM EFFECTS WHICH WILL STABILIZE THE GAME AT A LEVEL ABOVE THAT WHICH MIGHT OTHERWISE PREVAIL IN A CLOSED-EARTH MARKET. SUCH EFFECTS IF COMMENCED, WILL BE REGARDED AS NORMAL FOR ANY WOMB PLANET EXPERIENCING INTERSTELLAR BIRTH.

THE INVESTMENT

The Starseed Exchange (Starseed) will fabricate to order a High Orbital Mini Earth (H.O.M.E.) for any group desirous of living, working, playing and evolving in a world of their own design. A cooperative stock company will be formed by the underwriter for any such group, and the shares in each such company so formed may be traded on the Starseed Exchange.

Each H.O.M.E. will be a complete ecosystem manufactured from the finest extraterrestrial materials available, and built to exacting gravitational, climatic and environmental specifications, in keeping with the philosophy, cosmology, political system, epistemology, ethics, aesthetics, ontology and eschatology selected

STARSEED is engaged in the satisfaction of political, social, economic, technological and environmental desires.

by the migrants. As each H.O.M.E. is a self-supporting free-enterprise voluntary gene-pool without tax subsidy or other support from Old Earth governments, it will be wholly self-financed. Some H.O.M.E.s may choose to associate with one of the many ongoing ventures (see The Company) in the Personal Service, Information, Resort-Entertainment, Energy or Materials Groups. Others will spread through the solar system, taking charters, performing scientific missions, or engaging in venturesome exploration. Still other H.O.M.E.s may develop propulsion systems for leaving the solar system on interstellar voyages.

The cost of a H.O.M.E. will be equal to or less than the cost of earth homes of the same quality for a similar population. This offering is for the construction of H.O.M.E.s of the $300,000 per dwelling style, roughly comparable to 5,000 family dwellings in any American suburb, and similarly situated. It should be noted that STARSEED will also manufacture H.O.M.E.s of any size, shape, climate, gravitation or environment for any group. The partnership shares in any H.O.M.E. may be closely held, or traded on the STARSEED EXCHANGE.

THE COMPANY

High Orbital Mini Earths (H.O.M.E.s) are directly descended from primitive biological systems evolved in interstellar space and brought to this planet by meteorites about three billion years ago (see Hoyle and Wickramasinghe). STARSEED is engaged in the satisfaction of political, social, economic, technological and environmental desires, as follows:

PERSONAL SERVICE GROUP
H.O.M.E. Construction Division: Manages the design, development, fabrication and furnishings of H.O.M.E.s, luxurious miniworlds with multiple gravity, tailored eco-system, adjust-a-matic climate and free energy.

Tourism Division, dba "Head Trips Unlimited": Arranges transportation and accommodations for recreational visitors from the Old World. Also runs amusement parks and orbital docking facilities.

Medical Division: Provides longevity treatment for migrants, while operating Select-O-Gee convalescent complex and the Total Isolation Labs for genetic research.

Resort-Entertainment Division: Operates the Genetic Broadcasting Company and its stations WRNA and KDNA. Artists are brought together with the materials and environments of space under the Udall Fellowship program.

Do we not find exactly that for which we search?

INFORMATION GROUP:

Communication Division: Offers solar system wide telephone and data communication services. Planet-face features include global telephone service via satellite-linked wrist radio for US 25¢ per call regardless of time or distance.

Remote Sensing: Provides environmental and resource mapping and surveillance services across entire frequency spectrum at lower cost than planet-face systems.

Navigation/Location Division: Locates users precisely in timespace for purposes of sub-surface, surface, aerial and personal movement relative to precise coordinate systems.

Sensor Polling Division: Remote instantaneous polling of individual, group or automated terminals or sensors. Formerly the Gallup/Roper/Harris Division. Computer networks linking individuals throughout the Solar System.

ENERGY GROUP:

Solar Power Division: Constructs and maintains solar power satellites supplying pollution-free electrical power at 1 mil/KW hour to earth below the cost of fossil fuels.

Rent-a-Lumen Division: Rents light-time to areas of the earth desiring additional illumination at high or low intensities for social, agricultural or hedonic purposes.

MATERIALS GROUP:

Raw Materials Division: The Luna Station operated by this Division furnishes lunar soil to the space refineries by mass driver. Additional raw materials are provided to the refineries by the Asteroid Prospecting and Retrieval Teams in the form of carbonaceous chondrite asteroids.

Vapor Deposition Division: Vapor-Phase fabricates massive structures and thin-film solar sails of any size, shape and material. Formerly the Henson/Drexler Divison of Engulf and Devour, Inc.

Structural Materials Division: Produces immiscible alloys, float zone refined and directionally solidified castings, joinings and composites.

Process Materials Division: Produces catalysts, membranes, powders and devices in zero-to high gravity environments. Also provides hyper-pure materials refined in space.

Optical Division: Produces fibers, lenses, filters and other optical specialty devices. Grows crystals of any required purity, structure and dimension.

Biological Division: Separates, purifies and cultures the numerous pharmaceuticals and industrial chemicals which are produced most cost-effectively in zero-g environments.

Superior Intelligence is us in the future.

WARNING: THE GENETICS EXCHANGE COMMISSION REQUIRES THAT THE FOLLOWING WARNING MESSAGE BE IMPRINTED IN LARVAL SYMBOL UNITS ON EACH MUTATIONAL MESSAGE.

Your Genetic Director has determined that
MIGRATION
has reliably resulted, throughout evolution, in
METAMORPHOSES,
change in the individual, and
MUTATIONAL
change in the species.

The STARSEED EXCHANGE must also warn potential investors to seriously consider the possible effects on their own nervous systems of living for 150-800 years in a reality of their own design, with controlled weather, multiple gravities and free energy.

COMPETITION

The field in which STARSEED intends to function is highly competitive, as higher intelligences from at least 100,000 star systems in our galaxy are most assuredly engaged in the same business. Such entities may possess far greater experience, finances and facilities than the solar system or STARSEED.

It is recognized that in the broad sense, STARSEED will be competing not only with other producers of homes (Kaiser-Aetna, Irvine, ITT-Leavitt) but also with all producers, manufacturers and promoters of alternative realities (Earthfirst, Oneworld, Small is Beautiful, Limitgrowth and the Club of Rome). Additionally, competition may be considered to be present from all individuals and groups promoting the viewpoint that the highpoint of evolutions is larval forms stuck in two-dimensional planet-space who live less than 100 planet cycles.

SALES

STARSEED will solicit sales through various self-selecting mutational agents scattered over the planet-face who, through whatever means or media, gather a group to construct a H.O.M.E.

Although few such groups presently exist, the Company's past experience in promoting such ventures under the sponsorship of the DNA code, leads it to believe that it will be back-ordered above its projected ten (10) year capacity within six months. Such past ventures include the Plymouth Bay Space Colony, the East India Migration Company, and the Hudson Bay Extraterrestrial Trading Company.

Space Migration, Intelligence Increase, Life Extension.

EMPLOYEES AND PROMOTERS
The Company's founder and promoter (the DNA code) presently employs and promotes all life on the planet.

LEGAL MATTERS
To the best of anyone's knowledge, it is.

RISK FACTORS TO BE CONSIDERED
A. Although the Company was incorporated over four billion years ago on this planet, it has only been conscious of being conscious for a few thousand years.

B. Although the Company offers solutions to the four major systematic dilemmas of the species (growth, control, distribution and global uniformity) there is no assurance that the limited species consciousness of prevailing gene-pool interests will respond.

C. Although the ideas suggested herein are drawn from the work of the most evolved minds in the solar system, including higher intelligence from Princeton, MIT, Stanford, NASA, the aerospace community and our leading futurists and philosophers, and supported by years of study and reams of scientific data, most gene-pools would rather ignore these ideas than validate them in their own nervous systems.

D. Since it will be fun to live in space, get smarter, richer and live longer while evolving into a new interstellar species . . .

why not?

It took George A. Koopman eight years to found the American Rocket Company (AMROC). Its mission: to ferry equipment and people into low orbit.

During these years George founded a lecture agency, Future Presentations, which sent distinguished speakers around the country inpregnating minds with Space Migration memes. George also served as Special Effects Producer for the movie "The Blues Brothers" which starred John Belushi and Dan Ackroyd as Elwood and Jake, two cheerful guys "on a mission from God." George's assignment: to drop a Pinto (containing two Nazis) from a helicopter onto Daley Plaza in Chicago.

The first two full-sized AMROC rocket engines tested at Edwards Air Force Base in California (December 1986) were named "Elwood" and "Jake."

The most successful rocket engine testing in 1987 was immortalized by appearing on the cover of *Aviation Week & Space Technology*, the prestigious aerospace magazine. The name of this rocket engine was "Doctor Tim."

> The business of AMROC is the transportation of payloads to and from Earth orbit . . . By sacrificing the race-car performance of military missiles for the cost-efficiency of a delivery van, a family of industrial rockets can be produced and launched rapidly, safely, economically.

A few months before the first rocket launch a most splendidly endowed, super-fortunate, beautiful baby girl, Jane, arrived to join the ecstatic parents, George and Jacqui Koopman.

George and Jacqui and Jane we're all so proud of you all!

The following document is a memo issued in February 1988 by the American Rocket Company, George A. Koopman, President.

THE AMERICAN ROCKET COMPANY
Business Plan Summary

The business of the American Rocket Company (AMROC) is the transportation of payloads to and from Earth orbit—a package delivery service to outer space. To provide this service, AMROC will manufacture and operate its own industrial launch vehicles (ILVs). By sacrificing the race-car performance of military missiles for the cost-efficiency of a delivery van, a family of industrial rockets can be produced and launched rapidly, safely and economically.

Demands for space transportation service are expanding dramatically, especially for payloads to low Earth orbit. The growth is resulting from a combination of payload backlogs created by problems with existing launch systems, Federal policy that requires all US Government users to buy launch services rather than vehicles, and new markets created by developing technologies.

The large and growing backlog of payloads and serious delays for all users of space transportation are highlighted by the loss of Challenger and problems with the Titan, Delta, Atlas and Ariane systems. Government sponsored space and re-entry tests, NASA experiments, remote sensing and communications satellites, and commercial materials processing systems are all backing up due to unavailability of or delays in procuring launches. Further, NASA, which has been the primary US launch supplier, is now prohibited by national policy from seeking any new commercial payloads or maintaining a fleet of launch vehicles.

New markets for launch services are arising from developments in materials processing in space, remote sensing, communications satellites, service and product deliveries to future space stations, and a variety of other innovative applications in space.

A dozen market categories are projected for vehicles within AMROC capabilities by the late 1980s. Markets resulting from payload backlogs exist now and are projected to grow. Major new markets for on-orbit supplies will open in the early 1990s. Hundreds of orbital and sub-orbital launches will be required to meet known and projected needs that can be served by commercial enterprise before 1993.

AMROC's planned family of ILVs can perform a wide range of sub-orbital and orbital missions representing a full-service space transportation business, beginning with a revenue-producing single module sub-orbital system.

The US policy, legal and regulatory structures to support and encourage the private launch business are in place. AMROC principals have been central participants in the creation of these structures. Private launch-service development enjoys the specific encouragement of both the executive and legislative branches of the government. A new National Space Policy designed specifically to encourage, support, and assist private sector space commercialization was recently issued by the White House.

AMROC's US commercial competition is either using hardware derived from military vehicles, which fixes costs at high levels, or proposing new technologies requiring hundreds of millions of dollars to develop and demonstrate. Internationally, the space programs of France, China, Japan, and the USSR will provide launch services, but are restricted from servicing much of the US market by export controls and procurement policies.

AMROC's technical approach to industrial launch vehicles includes modular expendable launch systems utilizing nearly identical hybrid engines which are easily, quickly, and safely manufactured. Hybrid engines employ solid rubber-like fuel burned by adding a liquid oxidizer from a separate tank. The proposed launch system is environmentally clean and not subject to explosive failure. Other key technologies include a novel composite material for structural applications, glass filament-wrapped tanks and chambers, and use of recent advances in microelectronics and computers for guidance, navigation, control, and autopilot.

AMROC's planned family of industrial launch vehicles (ILVs) can perform a wide range of sub-orbital and orbital missions representing a full-service space transportation business, beginning with a revenue-producing single module sub-orbital system.

The financial strategy is to use AMROC's cost and availability advantage to enter the market at substantially below current launch prices. Low facilities costs maximize initial profit within a minimum launch schedule. Substantial margins will allow further price competition, and the opportunity to lower the price of services in exchange for participation in developing space ventures.

AMROC is currently building full size rocket engines at its plant in Camarillo, California and testing them and associated vehicle systems at the Air Force Astronautics Laboratory, Edwards Air Force Base, California. Vehicle system design, procurement and production for the first two vehicles are progressing in parallel.

A launch complex capable of supporting AMROC's suborbital and orbital launches is being prepared for 1988 operations at Vandenberg Air Force Base,

---

AMROC is the first private launch company to negotiate the use of national rocket test and launch facilities. While AMROC leases facilities from and will sell launch service to the US Government, we will not produce rockets as a government contractor.

California. AMROC is the first private launch company to negotiate the use of the national rocket test and launch facilities. While AMROC leases facilities from and will sell launch service to the US Government, we will not produce rockets as a government contractor.

AMROC will initially demonstrate its ability to provide commercial service by launching two sub-orbital test flights from Vandenberg Air Force Base, California starting in Fall, 1988, and by delivering a payload to low Earth orbit in 1989. AMROC may also provide the capability to return payloads from orbit, and may fly an automated flyback spacecraft on the third commercial orbital flight. Several US companies have built approximately five hundred of these flyback spacecraft which have flown US reconnaissance missions back from space with extremely high reliability.

Revenue-producing services will begin with sub-orbital launches in late 1988 and incorporate orbital and advanced sub-orbital vehicles by 1990, at which time the launch rate will reach one per month. By 1993, launches will reach one per week in all classes. After the initial test launches, AMROC will manufacture launch vehicles adjacent to its primary launch site, perhaps near Cape Canaveral, Florida, or on the island of Hawaii.

The AMROC team includes recognized leaders in the technologies specific to this plan, and successful engineers and managers of large and complex US space projects. The team has previously demonstrated the use and integration of these technologies. Members include founders and key personnel of Arc Technologies which designed, produced and launched American's first privately developed commercial rocket.

American Rocket Company was incorporated in California in May 1985. Shares were issued to the founders, Koopman, Bennett and McKinney.

During 1985, preliminary engine and ILV designs, a development plan, and a business plan were produced. The core team was recruited. Negotiations were conducted with the US Air Force for the use of its Astronautics Laboratory (AFAL), Edwards AFB, California.

During 1986, private placements were made of Series A Preferred Stock and Convertible Notes. Designs for the ILV-1 launch vehicle, including engines, vehicle structure, and guidance and control systems were modeled and tested. In February, AMROC moved into a light industrial facility in Menlo Park, California. In April an Agreement with the Air Force was concluded providing engine test facilities. In May, the first scale hybrid rocket engines designed and produced by AMROC were tested at AFAL. Sixteen firings of ten test engines were conducted between May and August 1986. A development plan and

The first orbital launch with a revenue payload on board will occur in 1989.

preliminary manufacturing plan were produced. In August, the complete launch system passed a comprehensive concept design review by a panel of outside experts.

In December 1986, AMROC conducted two tests of a full sized main engine. Two additional main engines were built and tested in early 1987 [Doctor Tim]. In April 1987, AMROC moved into a 22,000 sq. ft. production facility in Camarillo, California.

During 1987, private placements of Series B and C Preferred Stock raised funds for additional testing and production of the first flight weight engine, and for order deposits on long-lead guidance and communication items.

In October 1987, AMROC commenced tests of flight-sized 70,000 lb. thrust main engines, to our knowledge the largest hybrid motors ever built.

In November 1987, AMROC encountered difficulties following "Black Monday" as some investors failed to meet commitments, and was forced to suspend operations.

In December 1987, new financing allowed operations to resume. During December a flight size main engine was built in nine days and fired five times by January 8, 1988. A majority of AMROC's employees have now been called back to work. Three new test engines are currently in production. Two new test stands are being built at AFAL, and renovation work has resumed at AMROC's launch complex at Vanderberg AFB.

A private placement is currently underway to provide additional funds to flight test a single hybrid module, produce integrated hardware/software for full flight simulation of guidance and control, and complete design for the sub-orbital and small orbital vehicles.

A single module ILV will be launched on a sub-orbital test flight from Vandenberg AFB in the fall of 1988. A second ILV flight will likely carry a revenue producing payload at year's end.

Following the first sub-orbital flight test, major financing will be secured through private placement, corporate partners, or public offering. The first orbital launch with a revenue payload on board will occur in 1989.

ONWARD CHRISTIAN SOLDIERS:

A Brief History of the Warrior Caste in America

Esquire magazine says war is the secret love of a white man's life. The cover of its November 1984 issue shows a gorgeous young white woman wearing a Marine helmet and torn brown GI T-shirt.

The effect was sexually ambiguous, but steamy!

Great coverlines: "It is a sexual turn-on . . . it is a brutal, deadly game, but the best game there is. It is for men what childbirth is for women. It is like lifting the corner of the universe and looking at what is underneath."

Esquire's motto is: "Man at His Best." The title of the November '84 cover story: "Why Men Love War." The subhead was lyric: "The Awesome Beauty, the Haunting Romance, of the Timeless Nightmare." The piece was written by William Broyles Jr., a white, Protestant ex-Marine from Texas, who makes a good living these days refighting the Vietnam War in magazines and glorifying the enduring addiction of the American Warrior Caste and its sponsor, the Republican Party, to killing colored people with high-technology weapons.

The ESQUIRE piece appeared just when Reagan was lobbying to bully our Latin neighbors—once again. It's a recurrence of that old Caribbean fever, a paroxysmal virus that plagues the White House. Apparently, the Oval Office can't be disinfected. President after president keeps coming down with the Latin-basher disease.

When Ronald Reagan was elected President in 1980, everyone knew he was itching and feverish to send American troops into action. Somewhere. He just had to stand tall and bully some Third World country to regain the American manhood that General William Westmoreland says we lost in Vietnam.

But where to conduct a nice, little, easy-to-win, ego-massaging war?

The Russkis? Too mean.

Asians? The slopes proved too tough for MacArthur in Korea and for Westmoreland in Nam.

The Middle East? Much too volatile. Ronnie blustered a bit in Lebanon, but pulled out quickly after wasting the lives of hundreds of U.S. military personnel.

It started with the Spanish Conquistadors. The first Europeans to subdue Cuban, Nicaraguan and South American natives for Christ and Plunder were the Spanish.

Oh, well, back to the old, familiar playground for the Republican Party and the Warrior Caste. Let's snuff some Latins for God and manhood.

Cuba? Too risky.

Grenada was fun for a warm-up, but short and limited and easy.

Hmmm . . . Well, there's always good old Nicaragua. Since the 1890s the American military has occupied or controlled this least-populated nation in Central America. And for almost a century guerilla forces there have opposed American intervention. In 1933 we pulled out our occupation troops and set up a puppet dictatorship run by the Somoza family. The younger Somozas were proteges of the American Warrior Caste. Anastasio Somoza Debayle, for example, graduated from the U.S. Military Academy, returned home and, at age 21, took command of the National Guard. Because of the brutality of this regime, all democratic elements of the Latin World despised us. In 1979 the Sandinistas overthrew the Somozas, to the dismay of their academy classmates.

It started with the Spanish Conquistadors. The first Europeans to subdue Cuban, Nicaraguan and South American natives for Christ and Plunder were the Spanish. In 1493 Christopher (Christ-Carrier) Columbus returned to the New World with a disorderly rabble of male buccaneers seeking gold. It was hard going. No quick payoff. So, to man his third expedition in 1498, Columbus was forced to impress hooligans, convicts, rapists and thieves. An ominous precedent.

The next centuries of Spanish intervention were not designed to raise the morale of Caribbean natives, who were immediately looted, raped, baptized and reduced to serfdom by hoodlums representing Crown and Church. The Spanish settlements were rigidly controlled by Madrid. The colonists were the scum of Europe—soldiers, priests and plunderers. Black Africans were kidnapped to work as slaves.

Few Spanish women were involved in the first expeditions; so there was much forcible interbreeding with Indian and black slave women. This ancient custom produced the rich mestizo races, which now people these fertile lands. On the upside, Latin America was at least spared the shameful genocidal policies that characterized the North American colonization. I guess it's better to rape 'em and enslave 'em than to waste 'em.

When the South American countries gained independence from Spain, the feudal-military-Catholic traditions remained. Thus was created the unstable, volatile, romantic cultural environment that has left Latin America masochistically vulnerable to enduring and relentless Yankee adventuring.

> "Esquire's" ex-Lieutenant Broyles tells us that he and his Marine Corps buddies adored Vietnam because war "offers a sanction to play boys' games."

The Republican Party and the Warrior Caste love war. *Exquire's* ex-Lieutenant Broyles tells us that he and his Marine Corps buddies adored Vietnam because war "offers a sanction to play boys' games."

. . . Because "war replaces the difficult gray areas of daily life with an eerie, serene clarity."

. . . Because "war is the best game there is."

. . . Because "no sport I had ever played brought me to such deep awareness of my physical and emotional limits."

. . . Because the "love of war stems from the union, deep in the core of our being, between sex and destruction, beauty and horrow, love and death."

. . . Because some youths "who never suspected the presence of such an impulse in themselves have learned in military life the mad excitement of destroying."

. . . Because war is funny. "After one ambush my men [sic] brought back the body of a North Vietnam soldier. I later found the dead man propped against some C-ration boxes. He had on sunglasses, and a *Playboy* magazine lay open in his lap; a cigarette dangled jauntily from his mouth; and on his head was perched a large and perfectly formed piece of shit.

"I pretended to be outraged, since desecrating bodies was frowned on as un-American and counterproductive. But it wasn't outrage I felt. I kept my officer's face on, but inside I was . . . laughing."

Believe me, ex-Lieutenant Broyles, the people who founded our country—thoughtful men such as Thomas Jefferson and Ben Franklin—would not have considered this funny. Nor would three billion non-Caucasians with whom we share the planet.

How an Indian Chieftain's head ended up on a pole in Massachusetts. In the early 17th century, New England was controlled by a wise and benevolent leader. His friends called him Massasoit. In 1620 the first wave of immigrants from Europe started arriving in the lands of Massasoit. The original Plymouth colony was dominated by a Moral Minority, a small sect of fanatic Fundamentalist Protestants. These Puritans were regenerate (born-again) Christians who held a strict Calvinist belief in "the Elect *vs.* the Damned" and who publicly confessed their conversion experiences. These militant Protestants doggedly believed that human nature was inherently sinful and evil.

Over the decades the actions of the Republican Party can only be understood if we recall that they were bred to the terrible notion of being the Elect of God. Ronald Reagan deeply believes that there can be no mercy for nonbelievers. Those who are not "one of us" deserve no pity. Remember how Ronnie called

When the Puritans showed up in Plymouth, they considered it their right and religious duty to plunder the land of the heathen Pequot Indians. Poor King Massasoit! He wasn't ready for a Jesse Helms approach.

the Democrats "immoral" when they didn't vote for his military budget? Recall how he gives bloodcurdling sermons about the need to destroy Godless communism? That's not election rhetoric. The guy believes it. He really feels that he and his military friends are agents of God.

When the Puritans showed up in Plymouth, they considered it their right and religious duty to plunder the land of the heathen Pequot Indians. Poor King Massasoit! He wasn't ready for a Jesse Helms approach. In all good faith he had signed a peace treaty in 1621, to which he and his son, King Philip, faithfully adhered for 50 years in spite of continued land-grabbing by the white settlers.

In 1675 a typical colonial-liberation war broke out. King Philip's forces successfully avoided pitched battles and kept the conflict going until the European invaders, using "search and destroy" methods with the help of local *contras*, overthrew the native government. Philip, betrayed by a Christian convert, was drawn and quartered, and his head stuck on a pole in front of the church in Plymouth. This is known as the *final solution*.

It was all right, you understand, because these heathens were already damned. In the 365 years since the Pilgrims landed at Plymouth Rock, the Holy War faction of the white, spiritual fathers of the Republican Party has kept up a continual series of expansionist crusades against people with darker skins.

Indeed, for the born-again militants it has become a tradition, a rite of passage, a religious ritual. This is not just my opinion; Mr. Broyles agrees.

They admit it's a religious kick. In *Esquire*, William Broyles tells us that war provides aesthetic and religious ecstasies. He recounts the case of a "sensitive" Marine officer who watched enemy bodies being disposed of "like so much garbage" with a "look of creative contentment on his face that I had not seen except in *charismatic churches*. It was the look of a person transported into ecstasy.

"War is beautiful," Broyles gushes. "There is something about a firefight at night... brilliant patterns that seem, given their great speeds, oddly timeless, as if they had been etched in the night." Here Broyles soars into elegant gourmet connoisseurship. "Many men loved napalm... I preferred white phosphorous."

Intoxicated by this toot of white phosphorous, ex-Lieutenant Broyles invokes his white Calvinist divinity. "And then perhaps the gunships called Spooky come in and fire their incredible guns like huge hoses washing down from the sky, like something God would do when He was really ticked off."

Here we have the official Republican-Warrior Caste version of the Christian God: a vengeful colonial deity casually wasting Third World peasants who irritate Him. The Elect and the Damned.

> The Warrior Caste in America—the generals, the admirals, the cops—is overwhelmingly Republican. This is ominous. George Marshall, the only famous Democratic general of this century, is most renowned for his plans to wage peace.

The Republican Party is the Warrior Caste. The Republican Party, white and very Protestant, has always represented the buccaneer tradition in America.

The Democratic Party, by and large, represents the anti-Warrior constituency. During this century Democrats have been the party of progressives, Catholics, scientists, intellectuals, agnostics, Jews, blacks, Latins—minority groups that have always been barred from the highest ranks of the military.

In the 1985 budget fight it was the Republicans who wanted to cut social-educational programs and the Democrats who wanted to trim the military funds.

The Warrior Caste in America—the generals, the admirals, the cops—is overwhelmingly Republican. This is ominous. George Marshall, the only famous Democratic general of this century, is most renowned for his plans to wage peace.

This linkage of the GOP and the Warrior Caste is not new. From the Civil War through Eisenhower, seven out of 12 Republican Presidents have been ex-generals or glamorous Warriors.

This tradition of the Warrior President goes back to the beginning. George Washington, the Father of our Country, won his first fame in the Indian Wars.

It is important to note that the other "Father of Our Country," Thomas Jefferson, the spiritual founder of the Democratic Party, was an antimilitarist. It was Jefferson who framed the philosophic and legal documents that led to the Revolution and who wrote the Declaration of Independence.

A Jeffersonian President makes a sensible proposal to avoid war with Europe. President James Monroe, a disciple of Jefferson, is known for the treaties and diplomatic accords with England, France and Spain that managed to expand American interests without war. The Monroe Doctrine is his most famous achievement. There were two important and interdependent clauses in this manifesto. The first was a formal restatement of America-first neutrality. Beware of foreign entanglements! America promised not to intervene in European and (implicitly) Asian politics. In return, America declared the New World off limits for European intervention.

Modern American Presidents such as Kennedy and Reagan are on solid historical ground when they object to Russian meddling in Cuba and Central America. We all want to ban Soviet weapons from the New World. But Reagan is in direct violation of the Monroe Doctrine when he turns around and meddles in conflicts of the Old World. Arms to Pakistan and Turkey! More than 200,000 U.S. troops in Germany! Forty thousand in Korea! Marines landing in Lebanon to protect our oil interests!

Beware of foreign entanglements!

The filibuster President. *"Filibuster: . . . An adventurer who engages in a private military action in a foreign country . . . (originally 'freebooter,' . . . from Dutch* vrijbuiter, *pirate, 'one who plunders freely.' "*

The classic device of using a foreign adventure (the filibuster) as a stepping stone to the Presidency was invented by Andrew Jackson. In 1818 Jackson, then a major general, was sent off to Florida to campaign against the Seminole Indians. These natives, employing standard liberation tactics, fled across the border to Spanish Florida. Disregarding his orders, Jackson invaded Spanish territory and wasted various natives. He also executed two British subjects. Jackson's own private war created an international crisis. Responsible American officials denounced the action, but Jackson's illegal wog-bashing won support from populists, expansionists, ultra-nationalists, imperialists and Calvinist Protestants looking for a crusade against the heathens.

Jackson rode a wave of personal popularity that almost won him the Presidency in 1824. In 1828 he swept into office, and for two terms was able to use his populist Western support to protect Eastern financial interests. Sound familiar?

Is it a condition of manhood to love war? In his *Esquire* piece, which passionately glorifies the mechanized mass murder of Orientals, ex-Marine William Broyles Jr. is less than scientific. He writes, "Most men who have been to war would have to admit, if they are honest, that somewhere inside themselves they loved it . . . loved it as much as anything that happened to them before or since."

But wait a minute. Isn't ex-Lieutenant Broyles describing a well-known altered state of consciousness that can be and usually is attained by many other less-violent means?

The scientific situation seems to be something like this. There are circuits in the human brain that when activated produce heightened states of awareness. Among these are certain neutral tracts, mainly centered in the midbrain, which mediate convulsive survival behavior. These ancient primitive circuits are involved in fight, flight, territorial defense and male dominance. When one is engaged in violence, one falls into a trance-like state that produces an incredible adrenaline rush. Some call this the mad-dog reflex, or going berserk.

This sympathetic nervous system hit is necessary for our survival repertoire. It's like the endorphin-opiate rush that protects us from pain. Useful for survival, but dangerously addictive.

At this point we must remind ex-Lieutenant Broyles that the Destructive

> **Bullies love to express their manhood by riding in male-bonded packs. Gangs in the ghetto feel it. The Waffen SS feel it. It's called "warrior love."**

Paroxysmal State (DPS), which he glamorizes and politicizes, is not restricted to war.

We have all felt on occasions this seductive invitation to "flip-out" in wild destructiveness. You don't have to ship eight million young Americans 8,000 miles across the Pacific to waste a small Asian country. Catch a barroom brawl in a Burt Reynolds-Clint Eastwood movie. Tune into a prime-time TV show like *The A-Team.*

Alcohol trips off the DPS. Drop into any redneck saloon in Texas. Visit a clinic for battered wives, ex-Lieutenant Broyles, and you'll get a glimpse of your favorite "corner of the universe." Put on some black leather and join a bikers' club. Bullies love to express their manhood by riding in male-bonded packs. Gangs in the ghetto feel it. The Waffen SS felt it. It's called "warrior love."

From the halls of Montezuma to the shores of Tripoli . . . The Mexican War (1846-48) is another good example of the fun-fame-fortune rewards of Latin-bashing. After the conflict Mexico conceded two-fifths of its land to America.

The Mexican War was a bonanza for the Warrior Caste and for ambitious Republican politicians. Take Zachary Taylor. For starters, he earned his general's stars by snuffing Sac, Fox and Seminole Indians, for which he won the label "Old Rough and Ready." His Mexican War triumphs assured him the Presidency at the age of 65.

General Winfield Scott had good wog-busting credentials. He fought the Creeks and the Seminoles and "supervised the removal of the Cherokee to the Southwest." Scott won the battle of Mexico City and proceeded to defy the U.S. envoy during the peace negotiations, causing considerable embarrassment in Washington. Agents of God shouldn't have to obey diplomatic rules; Reagan and Ollie North understand that.

The recent rehabilitation of the freebooter ethos. How, we wonder, can a presumably respectable journalist like William Broyles get away with a cover story in *Esquire* celebrating the wanton, lustful slaying of millions of Asians in the name of self-fulfillment? Well, it turns out the Broyles, for self-esteem and profit, is shrewdly surfing the wave of neo-militarism generated by the Reagan regime.

During the Vietnam fiasco and "Give Peace a Chance" antiwar movement of the '60s, and during the human-rights moments of the Carter period, the Puritan-killer ethic got pushed around a bit. But it never disappeared. The Reynolds-Eastwood hero figures were still packing them into the theaters. The Reagan Administration enthusiastically rehabilitated militarism. The adventurist

---

This Christian-soldier stuff is not limited to the redneck South and Southwest. It plays well all around white, Calvinist America. The American Legion, the NRA, Hell's Angels, the Marine Corps Association, the survivalists, the G. Gordon Liddy crowd . . .

---

hero was back in the saddle! Wog-bashing was back in style. It was the triumphant return of the Wild West pirate who scornfully ignores the legalities of effete politicians and takes the law into his own hands.

[This intimidation of IranScam was written in 1984.] Lieutenant Calley, you're forgiven. The heroes of My Lai are marching down Fifth Avenue in a ticker-tape parade. Crank up Ollie North.

This Christian-soldier stuff is not limited to the redneck South and Southwest. It plays well all around white, Calvinist America. The American Legion, the National Rifle Association, the Hell's Angels, the Marine Corps Association, the survivalists, the G. Gordon Liddy crowd and *Soldier of Fortune* readers are visible tips of a profoundly deep American need to get kicks from wasting people.

A strange little episode in Nicaragua. William Walker (1824-60) merits a footnote in history as a classic case of an American Warrior compulsively involved in private, illegal plundering raids of Caribbean countries. In 1853 Walker led a group of frontier hoodlums in quest of Latin American plunder. First they tried Sonora, Mexico. The freebooting mission failed miserably. Walker was arrested for violation of neutrality laws. An understanding frontier American jury acquitted him. He was apparently a charismatic, John Wayne kind of guy. A good communicator, you might say. And after all, it was only Mexicans he had wasted.

In 1855 Walker joined a group of *contra* revolutionaries in Nicaragua. After overthrowing the government, Walker obtained recognition from the U.S. State Department and set himself up as dictator of Nicaragua. But the real power in Nicaragua those days was American tycoon Cornelius Vanderbilt, whose Accessory Transit Company monopolized trade in that inviting land. When Walker's operation became competitive, Vanderbilt ran him out.

But Walker still suffered from that old Caribbean freebooter disease, as recurrent as malaria. In 1860, based now in Honduras, he led still another pirate attempt to take over Central America. It failed, and Latin-basher William Walker was finally done in by a Honduran government firing squad, leaving behind a book that has some relevance today. It's called *War in Nicaragua*. [Three years after this essay (Onward Christian Soldiers) was written, Alex Cox released the movie, "Walker."]

The Communist Party Takes Over America

The American Civil War (1861-1865), the bloodiest conflict in history was provoked when a bully strong-man, Abraham Lincoln used federal troops to ruthlessly suppress the freedom of the southern states and force them

---

By 1898 the expansionists and war-lovers and the heretic-bashers had simply run out of poor neighbors to invade. A new generation of young men hungered for the "awesome beauty, haunting romance and time-less nightmare" of a colonial war. How 'bout a little rumble in Cuba?

unwillingly into the American Union. Before thie "Breznev maneuver," the USA was a loose confederation of small sovereign, agricultural states. Lincoln, as would Lenin, sixty years later, created a centralized, industrial, militaristic, expansionist government. Just as the Communist Party has managed the USSR since 1921, so has the Republican Party, USA, controlled the police, the military, the banks, the manufacturing plants, the organs of information.

This change from small, feudal agricultural states to a highly organized, mechanistic, imperialistic, monolithic, state-centered society is an inevitable stage in human evolution. The time had come for the industrialization-stage. In the eighty years after Lincoln and the Party seized control of America other smokestack countries—Japan, Germany, Italy, Russia, set up similar centralized military-industrial systems controlled by a "Party."

After the Civil War the Party leadership in the American Union automatically went to military men. U.S. Grant was succeeded by Major General Rutherford B. Hayes. Then Major General James Garfield, a lay preacher in the Disciples of Christ, was succeeded by Quartermaster General Chester A. Arthur. Pres. Benjamin Harrison was a brigadier General. All, of course, were party members.

It was during this stage of industrial-military growth that the glorification of the Warrior Caste hit its peak. Statues were raised in the center of every town and city: a general (and Party leader) on a bronze horse, riding as to war. With the Cross of Jesus going on before!

The religious issue just won't quit. Now comes *Esquire* magazine, publishing an inflammatory moral justification of warfare at a spooky moment in history when nuclear conflagration threatens and when the religious right-wing in thei country and in several Islamic theocracies speaks approvingly of Holy Wars, Evil Empires and Armageddons. Onward Christian Soldiers! It's another Crusade against Satan. It's Jihad time. Blow it all up for Allah! Kill for Kaddafi! Praise the Lord and pass the ammunition! Hand me that red phone, boy. Howdy there, God. Time to drop the Big One on the Godless heathens like the Good Book says!

Reflect for a moment on the quotes from the Broyles article. Glazed-eye babble about brotherly love among the napalm, and God as the gunner in a helicopter gunship, and blissed-out looks on the faces of charismatic Protestants, and the psychotic Marine assassin with "JUST YOU AND ME, LORD" tattooed on his shoulder.

Caribbean fever strikes again. The war for Southern independence ended in 1865. Between 1869 and 1878 more than 200 pitched battles were fought against a new invented enemy—the Plains Indians. The Massacre of Wounded Knee was the final solution for this overpopulation problem. More than 200

During the 20th century every generation of young Americans has been offered a foreign expeditionary war.

unarmed men, women and children were killed. "The soldiers later claimed that it was difficult to distinguish the Sioux women from the men," a complaint to be heard again in later wars against colored people.

By 1898 the expansionists and war-lovers and the heritic-bashers had simply run out of poor neighbors to invade. A new generation of young men hungered for the "awesome beauty, the haunting romance, the timeless nightmare" of a colonial war. Well, how about a little rumble in Cuba?

It so happened that there were heavy American investments to protect on the island. The military, with its eye on Panama and Nicaragua for a canal, stressed the strategic position of the island. It was easy for the press to whip up support for the *contras* fighting against Spain.

Cuba was a media war. William Randolph Hearst broadcast fake propaganda. There was a Gulf of Tonkin-Korean Air Lines Flight 007 faked incident involving the American battleship USS *Maine*.

The war itself was a pushover. The Spanish put up token resistance. The biggest winner was a wealthy politician named Teddy Roosevelt, who organized his own semiprivate regiment (Western cowboys and "adventurous bluebloods from Eastern universities") whose routine exploits were highly publicized. Quick results: Within three years Roosevelt—a swashbuckling, militaristic, Reagan-type—was in the White House. Roosevelt's regime was continually involved in Latin-bashing, dollar diplomacy, Venezuela and the Philippines. He infuriated all of Latin America by placing, in the Dominican Republic, U.S. customs officers who stole revenues for the benefit of American business. He backed a group of *contras* who hijacked Panama from Colombia. Just eight years ago, when Jimmy Carter returned the Canal to Panama, the Republicans screamed, "Treason! We stole that canal fair and square."

Roosevelt's jingoistic imperialism made him the scourge of Democrats, progressives and Jeffersonian Americans. And in 1906 Teddy, the ultimate war freak and ultra-imperialist, won the Nobel Peace Prize. Shades of Henry Kissinger!

A busy time for the Warrior Caste. During the 20th century every generation of young Americans has been offered a foreign expeditionary war. World War I against the Huns. World War II against the Nazis and Japanese. To prop up the unspeakable fascist regime of South Korea, our generals sacrificed more than 50,000 American lives. General Douglas MacArthur, the ultimate freebooter, started to wage his own little psychotic war against a billion slant-eyed Chinese until he was forcibly removed by President Truman. "Dugout" Doug returned as a hero and announced his candidacy for the Presidency. On the Republican ticket, of course.

**My wife is worried about this article ... she thinks that I've gone too far ...
Her warning is well-taken; so let me explain ...**

Then came Vietnam. And Cambodia.

More explosives were dropped on Vietnam than during all of our 200 years of warfare. Not to mention a small sea of Agent Orange, which has left much of that unfortunate land blighted for years to come. We have listened recently to a deafening chorus of aggrieved complaints from Vietnam vets who feel unrewarded; we hear very little about the punishing casualties we inflicted upon the peoples of Vietnam and Cambodia. We won the Body Count War! We wasted 'em—soldiers, civilians, women and children.

Esquire is off to a good start. Let's encourage these psycho vets to tell their stories about the fun of body-desecration, and the "perfectly formed piece of shit" on the non-Caucasian's head, and "the mad excitement of destroying," and about how impossible it is to talk about it unless you were there. It's good Freudian catharsis. And let's build them a monument where they can weep, not for Vietnam and Cambodia wasted, not for America rent by conflict, not for Jeffersonian ideals lost, but in pity for themselves.

But the ticker-tape parade led by General Westmoreland isn't enough. Even cover stories in national magazines can't heal the scar of ex-Lieutenant Broyles. Even a full-page picture of him in natty suit and tie, looking very serious-grim like a young Dallas stockbroker, standing in front of a war memorial with his blond kid (a boy, of course) in his arms, holding (no shit) the American flag in front of an *enormous* bronze statue of three real young, clean-cut, good-looking white soldiers—Texas A&M types—raising still another American flag over Iwo Jima, Managua or even Havana?

Patriotism and the Christian soldiers. My wife is worried about this article. She thinks that I've gone too far. She fears that this expose of the Warrior Caste is going to sound unpatriotic. "America is a young country without traditions," she explains. "We need heroes and a glorious history."

Her warning is well-taken; so let me explain. I'm a total, all-out 101% patriot, Jack. I yield to no one in my contempt for socialism, communism or any enemy of freedom. I also believe in a strong, intelligent, effective military to defend our beloved land.

That's exactly why I oppose the Christian fanatics and the war-wing of the Republican Party. That's why I write about the con job that they have pulled off for the past hundred years.

As I review American history, I see a large glorious company of heroic men and women who represent our red-white-blue ideals of initiative, intelligence, tolerance, humor, compassion, common sense, optimism and good-natured

Hear this, lads: We have called off the Christian crusade. You don't have to bully others to prove your manhood.

---

skepticism of bureaucracy and authority. People who believe in fair play and who dislike armed bullies running around in uniforms.

Let's list a few examples of true American heroes—gentle William Penn, founder of Philadelphia, City of Brotherly Love; Henry David Thoreau, the Concord Libertarian; Edgar Allan Poe, a West Pointer who became a literary star; inventors such as Eli Whitney, Robert Fulton and Thomas Edison; Ralph Waldo Emerson, philosopher of self-reliance; Walt Whitman and Mark Twain.

Let's recall the long line of blacks who have provided us models of noble humanity, creatively waging peace not war—George Washington Carver, Ralph Bunche and Dr. Martin Luther King, Jr., among others.

The civilized American hero. What, indeed, is any thoughtful American going to feel when exposed to this American Legion, Born-Again fake patriotism?

Most of us—Catholics, Jews, blacks, Latins, women and men—came to the U.S. to escape militarism and to create a better social order. Basically, most of us don't want to stir up foreign adventures and turn our country into a Christian empire. We've got enough real problems here at home—the complicated transition from an industrialized economy; the agonizing racial tensions; the collapse of our education system. There is a need for heroes, not to lead religious crusades, but to apply goodwill, tolerance and intelligence to make the American Dream come true.

So let's issue some patriotic American commands to ex-Lieutenant Broyles and his comrades. *ABOUT FACE! ORDER ARMS! AT EASE!*

Hear this, lads: We have called off the Christian crusade. You don't have to bully others to prove your manhood!

A Common-Sense Plan
For the '88 Selection

Beverly Hills
January 1988

The 1988 selection is the first in which the entire cohort of the Post War generation gets to vote for president. If they share any minimal concensus, this enormous bloc of 78 million Baby Boom Americans (born between 1946 and 1964) will surely determine the next president. I happen to believe that these Americans now between the ages of 24 and 42 do, indeed, share a unique genetic imprint, a special "attitude." If this is true, and if it can be activated, then forget landslide when you think 88. Let's prepare for a democratic avalanche.

But, who can predict how this changeable and diverse group will vote? So far these pesky Post-War kids have certainly altered their tactics and styles from decade to decade. In the 50s they appeared as televoid "Mousketeers." In the 60s their mushy utopianism was branded "Hippy." In the 70s their libertarian activism was labeled "Yippy." In the 80s the media hook is "Yuppy"—as in Young Upscale Pragmatic.

We grant that attaching these journalistic buzz-words to 78 million individuals from Maine to Maui is not precise social science discourse. But still, behind the changing badges, are certain psycho-biological realities. The Dr. Spock people are measurably different from preceding generations. They were born into a TV-culture. They are better educated, information richer, more exposed, sophisticated. They are the first electronic, cybernetic human beings.

Also important is the fact that since their birth the Big Mushroom Clouds have hung over their pretty little heads. They are the first nuclear generation, the first of our breed to know that they can never, ever dress up in those flashy Boy Clout uniforms bedecked with ribbons and boisterously swagger off to celebrate the favorite whoopee, Rambo past-time of our species. War.

If they are anything, the Baby Boomers are Post Warriors.

The heroic fuzz-words of World War II, so sacred to us oldsters—Munich, Pearl Harbor, Patton, Rommel, Mussolini, G.I. Joe, Iwo Jima, Stalin, De Gaulle, George Marshall—are as alien to the Spockers as Ulysses Grant and Sgt. York. And the memories of post-war people are Chernobyl-burned with those horrid two words that we, their elders, fervently prefer to forget: Hiroshima-Nagasaki.

"Narcissistic" means they accept the Emersonian notion of self-reliance. They are independents. They are free agents. They accept responsibility for piloting their lives.

Unlike their parents and grandparents they grew up with no military idols or charismatic warrior role models. No generals on bronzed horseback will be built in their shopping malls. Nostalgia for former World War II heroics would have been rather kinky for the 50s Mousketeers whose parents were told to build bomb shelters in the basement. Does anyone remember?

And, after the failures of the American military in Korea, Vietnam and Beirut, the Post Warriors are overwhelmingly anti-militarist. They are certainly less than enthusiastic to "pay any price, bear any burden, meet any harsdhip" for Old Warriors dreams of martial glory.

To dramatize the effect of these demographics consider this fact. In the year 1998, ten years from now, over two-thirds of the members of the U.S. House of Representatives will have been fans of the Beatles and Bob Dylan thirty years before. Two-thirds will have sung, "Give Peace a Chance" and smoked pot. These adolescent imprints are permanently hard-wired to their hormones.

Interesting credentials for a new crop of voters?

IS IT ANY WONDER THAT THE POST WAR-RIORS HAVE BECOME PRACTICAL NO-NONSENSE REALISTS?

After what the Post-War-riors have been through—the 3-K assassinations, Watergate, Iranscam, Gary Hart, Jimmy Swaggart, and the sordid, squalid collapse of six straight presidencies—is it any wonder that they turn out to be a skeptical, tough-minded, realistic demographic group? Logically enough their life goals have matured. Surprise! They are now concerned with practical issues like pay-checks, education, physical and mental fitness, excellence, careers, homes, gourmet consumption and a peaceful, prosperous, sane world for their consciously-conceived, demand-bred, custom-designed kids.

Makes common sense, doesn't it?

We, their good-hearted but confounded elders who, ten years ago, had ridiculed them for being romantic, long-haired, hedonistic, impractical utopians, now denounce them for being politically apathetic, narcissistic materialists.

Let's perform a quick semantic analysis of these moralistic buzz-words.

"Politically apathetic" means they are skeptical about partisan politics and simplistic solutions.

"Narcissistic" means they accept the Emersonian notion of self-reliance. They are independents. They are free agents. They accept responsibility for piloting their lives. They think for themselves. They are self-indulgent and self-disciplined.

"Materialistic" suggests that they are tough-minded, street-smart, hip. They are zen warriors, *ronin*.

The 1988 presidential selection could well go to the team of candidates who speak street-smart pragmatics to the overwhelming majority of sensible Americans who want a calm, non-confrontational, friendly, realistic, non-divisive, business-like management team in Washington.

Culturally, they seem to be laissez-faire libertarians. They don't want the government or Rev. Marion (Pat) Robertson or the Pope, or even Nancy Reagan telling them how to manage their bodies or their personal lives. When they say "No, thank you to drugs" their polite refusal is pragmatic not emotional or moral. You see, they have to be alert (neither too wired nor too mellow) for that 8:30 meeting at the office.

This interesting new breed is too busy with life-planning to follow Abby Hoffman into the streets to protest. Unlike those reared in Belfast or the Lower East Side, outrage is not their typical adolescent mood. Neither is hysterical hand-wringing. These are veterans of Woodstock, you remember. They're basically cool. They've learned how to flip the channel. They pay the rent.

The polls show that most younger Americans are political independents. They realize that the country cannot win the pennant with screaming zealots in the dug-out. The operational question posed to a wanna-be leader is, "What's your batting average?"

The 1988 presidential selection could well go to the team of candidates who speak street-smart pragmatics to the overwhelming majority of sensible Americans (including most of the Post Warriors) who want a calm, non-confrontational, friendly, realistic, non-devisive, business-like, management team in Washington.

Hey, we have more than enough practical problems on our hands. It's a confusing task to convert our incredibly diverse country from a smokestack factory culture into a cybernetic 21st century nation. And how do you formulate a foreign policy with extremely young, immature, unsophisticated, insecure governments like the Soviet Union (b. 1922), Japan (b. 1947), South Korea (b. 1948), and Red China (b. 1949). Hey, there's some heavy juvenile delinquency here. How can virtuous, venerable Uncle Ron, the senile leader of the oldest, creakiest industrial democracy on the planet, deal with these crazy under-privileged, young punk adolescent nations which are growing unsightly nationalist pimples, swaggering around having teen-age identity crises in the UN?

SO WHO WILL WE SELECT IN 1988?

If the '88 "campaign" is "fought" along traditional "battle-lines," all of us stand to "lose."

Linguistic note. Reflect upon the ominous kamakazi words we use here. The game, you know, is played with ideas, words. And our words will select our leaders.

Michel Foucault and the French linguists suggest that we are imprisoned by

The media-hip, screen-smart Yuppy-vote might well go to the person who explicitly and articulately avoids re-runs of the photogenic actor or the huckster pitchman models—media hotdogs like Reagan, Robertson and Falwell could be made to look as outdated as Ed Sullivan.

our language. To the extent that this is true, are we not held political hostage by such terms as "win" and "campaign" and "fought" and lose"?

Do not these words conjure up images of war-chiefs or of wrestlers matched in hand-to-hand combat? Or even worse, old bulls goring each other for leadership of the flock or herd?

It is comically true that any American politician who volunteers to endure two years of highly publicized mouth-to-mouth combat in dismal Iowa and carnival mud wrestling in frigid New Hampshire should be instantly disqualified as some sort of clown who lacks emotional balance, mature dignity, self-respect and plain, damn common sense.

A second semiotic factor: television as medium of communication. Recent elections have been "won" as Oscars and Emmies are "won" on the basis of acting skills, plus money to buy the time for slick candidate commercials.

By '88 the media-hip, screen-smart Yuppy-vote might well go to the person who explicitly and articulately avoids re-runs of the photogenic actor or the huckster pitchman models. In the '88 selection media hotdogs like Reagan and Robertson and Falwell could be made to look as outdated as Ed Sullivan.

A third semiotic menace haunting the '88 selections is the very concept of the regal presidency itself. To "pre-side" means to sit before as on a throne.

The cybernetic 21st century Yup-scale vote might well go to the **coach** or **pilot** who offers us a **team** or **crew** and a pennant-winning game-plan or a business-like production-distribution blueprint or a no-bullshit flight-plan to navigate our nation profitably through the next stormy twelve years of Millennium Madness.

The observant reader will have noted that I am using a Foucault tactic here, slyly manipulating language, inserting the jargon of sports or navigation or bizarre Japanese words like "profit" in order to liberate the discussion from the shackles of Biblical or Cold Warrior terminology.

The political metaphors of the immediate future could well come from our favorite public ceremony, organized sports. Some of our deepest social yearnings are currently projected on and expressed through athletes and coaches. We expect our athletic models to admit mistakes, honestly praise opponents and modestly give credit for success to team-work and crowd support. A coach who incites moral hatred for opponents, who boasts, who cheats & lies, who claims victory in spite of the scoreboard totals would be laughed out of the league. In politics, however, such megalomaniac idiots run for our highest offices. And, too often, win.

Perhaps the '88 nominating conventions should be run like the NFL draft.

> Perhaps nominating conventions should be run like the NFL draft. The goal is not to "fight" for delegates, not to incite passions and paranoias through flowery speeches. The cool tactic is to draft and field a well-balanced team to compete with the Tokyo Tigers and the Moscow Bears.

The goal of the convention is not to "fight" for delegates, not to incite passions and paranoias through flowery speeches. The cool tactic is to draft and field a well-balanced team to compete with the Tokyo Tigers and the Moscow Bears.

If we continue the sports metaphor, it becomes clear that our home team, the USA, is in a slump. We no longer lead the league. We even trail Beggar-Brazil in the national-debt category. The solution is obvious. Let's not passively choose from the loud-mouth clowns who volunteer for the job. Let's aggressively go out there and draft or trade for top talent who can restore our winning tradition.

Who? Well, all the scouting reports indicate that there is one political super-star, the MVP (Most Valuable Politician) of the 1980s. This performer is respected, charismatic, efficient. He is Youngish. He's a Post Warrior. He wants to end the Arms Race. He's practical. He wants to reward free enterprise and quality job performance. He wants to open up and liberalize. He's faithful to his wife.

How about Mikhail Gorbachev for President?

But how can we get the Soviets to trade us this top star? If we offered them Bush and Dole and Gore they'd laugh. Throw in all of our candidates, even Gary Hart and some cash and the Persian Gulf and even Bill Cosby? No way. They're too shrewd to give us Gorby for our unproven minor-league rookies.

There is one trade possibility. It seems that the powerful conservative forces in the Soviet Union don't like Gorby. They felt more comfortable with old Breznev who kept the Cold War going and built up the military and ran a nice clean law and order regime.

And, good news! There is one American leader that the Soviet establishment would actually prefer to this brash youngster Gorby. There is one American leader who is, come to think of it, a genial Breznev clone. A nice senile, solid, old-fashioned Cold Warrior who loves parades and military bands and who would happily stand in uniform in Red Square and salute the tanks rolling by.

So, how about we make a straight-up player for player swap with the Soviets.

We get Mike Gorbachev for Player-Coach-President of the USA. Gorby immediately pardons Ronald Reagan and George Bush for their high crimes and misdemeanors.

Then, the Russkis sign up Ronald Reagan to be General Secretary of the Soviet Union.